T0077186

THE
DAREDEVIL
ENTREPRENEUR

The Journey and Teachings of
a Successful Entrepreneur

Thomas Gotshall

Order this book online at www.trafford.com
or email orders@trafford.com

Most Trafford titles are also available at major online book retailers.

Print information available on the last page.

ISBN: 978-1-4907-1922-1 (sc)
ISBN: 978-1-4907-1924-5 (hc)

Library of Congress Control Number: 2013920866

Trafford rev. 06/23/2015

 www.trafford.com

North America & international
toll-free: 1 888 232 4444 (USA & Canada)
fax: 812 355 4082

Contents

Preface

This was never intended to be a book. In fact it was intended for my eyes only. My dad died in March of 2004 and I felt a great loss after his death. Someone suggested I write about him, along with what I had learned about entrepreneurship from him over all those years. I needed a release and thought just maybe this would bring some sort of peace to me. Then, as I was writing, it dawned on me that this compiled information could be helpful to many budding entrepreneurs as well as to others such as parents who are trying to encourage their sons or daughters to take this path in life.

It is no easy task writing a book, especially because I'm not the author type. I'm a businessperson interested in the creation of enterprise. However my sister, Kathy, pushed me to write this because, in her opinion, the world would be better off with it. You see, my sister is very proud of me and what I have accomplished as an entrepreneur. She also felt that telling my story would be a way of sharing our dad's story as well. Now that you have this book or computer screen in your hands, I hope you enjoy reading it as much as I enjoyed writing it. I also hope you learn a lot and begin your own entrepreneurial quest. If my book simply motivates you to go after the dream, mission accomplished.

Acknowledgments

In addition to all my dad's teaching and insights, this book would not exist if not for my mom, Marian. Not only did she bring me into the world, she saved my life countless times. More on that later in the book. Also the following individuals were very helpful in the completion of this book:

Editors: Claudia Capos and Cathy Broberg.

My family: Marti, Kristen, Erica, and T.J.

My mom, Marian, and sister and brother, Kathy and Rob.

And this book is dedicated to my dad: Robert H. Gotshall Sr.

Introduction
Saving the World

Who do you think will lead and sustain the economic recovery?

The government?

Big business?

The unions?

None of the above. It will be the entrepreneur, period.

Entrepreneurs create small businesses that grow to medium then sometimes large corporations.

The government doesn't "create" anything. Politicians write laws and form policies. Some of these laws and policies help businesses grow; however, many more cost businesses money and therefore force cutbacks and more layoffs. Big business is trying to shrink and cut costs by reducing its workforce. Unions don't hire anybody. They want employees to join and pay dues. They profess the union will protect them and make sure their employers will treat them better. At one point in our history this was a much needed institution; however, for the most part, the need for union representation has passed.

The one thing that grows an economy is employment. As the recovery begins to take hold, it will be shrinking unemployment that will do it.

Our capitalist society depends on its citizens working, making, and spending money. It drives the housing industry, retail industry, automobile industry. In fact, all commerce is driven by its citizens *buying* things.

People with incomes will move every single industry in a positive direction. Today the world is one enormous economy, entirely dependent on its citizens being employed and purchasing products and services. It all starts with an individual entrepreneur implementing his or her dreams, then hiring others to make it happen. Consider the quote: "It takes a Village to raise a child." This can also be applied to an entrepreneur's dream: "It takes a Village to make a Business Thrive."

Examples:

- Sam Walton started with a neighborhood hardware store with 7 employees, and today Wal-Mart employs over 2,100,000.
- Bill Gates built his first computer by himself. Today, Microsoft employs 88,000.
- Tom Monahan made a pizza for home delivery, and today Domino's employs 145,000.
- Levi Strauss made a pair of rugged blue jeans in 1858. Today the company employs 22,000.

The list goes on and on. Every one of these companies started with an entrepreneurial vision and dream.

I, too, am an entrepreneur. I started at the age of ten under the guidance of my dad. Between my snow/lawn maintenance business, rental house painting, and finally my rental property business, I contributed to the employment of over 200 people.

This was before starting my company Technical Solutions Inc., which employed over 220 directly. Indirectly, the company contributed to the employment of over 1,000—vendors, suppliers, bankers, accountants, and lawyers.

You may or may not want to grow your idea to such heights, yet the possibility exists. The most important thing is you must start at the beginning just like every other successful entrepreneur has.

My book is divided into three sections:

- Part 1 describes my early years as an entrepreneur, including my character traits and situation that led me to enter this path.
- Part 2 focuses on the formation of other ventures and the creation and eventual sale of my largest enterprise to date, Technical Solutions.
- In part 3, I share more tips on becoming an entrepreneur based on my own experience. Here I cover the necessary building blocks and experience all entrepreneurs need to become successful.

I hope that my personal and professional insights will help in your own entrepreneurial quest. If my book saves you some time and enhances your knowledge, all the better. Thanks for reading and enjoy the ride.

Part I

My Father—Hero, Mentor, and Best Friend

1

Lunch with Dad

As a young adult, I met my dad, Robert Gotshall, for lunch one day. I thought it would be a one-time encounter. Certainly, neither of us ever figured it would turn into what it did—a journey that lasted for twenty years. Lunch with Dad took place every Friday and changed both of our lives forever.

It all began on a snowy Friday morning in southeast Michigan. When I got up that morning at 6:30, a five-inch blanket of fresh white snow already covered our city. It was cold, which meant that the snow was light and powdery. This storm started sometime after midnight, continued through rush-hour, and now looked as if it would last all day. The drive into work that morning took twice as long as normal, over an hour and a half. My dad and I happened to work in the same office complex, the Prudential Town Center, a series of five buildings tied together by a web of walkways and tunnels, located in Southfield, Michigan.

My dad worked for the U.S. Chamber of Commerce as their director of Marketing and Advertising. I was working for a computer company, MAI/ Basic Four, a public company with annual revenue of $400 million. After only three months on the job, I had just been promoted from sales assistant to sales executive. My "real" career was about to start. My dad's office had moved to the Town Center just a month earlier. Although we were in different buildings, we were connected by the tunnels.

The year was 1983, before cell phones and texting, so "land lines" were the standard form of communication. My administrative assistant paged me that morning. "Tom, your dad is on line 5 asking for you." I quickly picked up the phone. "Hi, Dad. Is everything okay?"

My dad hardly ever called me, especially at work. He replied, "I don't know about you, but I don't want to venture out in all that snow for lunch. How about we meet at Diamond Jim Brady's for a bite to eat?"

I replied "What a great idea. Neither of us has to even put a coat on and I am less than five minutes away by foot. Let's do it. See you in a few minutes."

Our relationship was different from many father/son relationships. While he did the normal dad stuff like help me with my homework, he also took me under his wing in another way. My dad took on the role of my entrepreneurial coach when I was still quite young. This meant, in part, that we spent more time talking about a range of topics than was common. However, when I became an adult, we sort of drifted apart. I was busy trying to get my post-college life rolling. He knew I was focused on this and that I had to figure it out on my own. He was well established in his work world but he was busy playing his other roles as well: husband to my mom, Marian, and father to my sister, Kathy, and brother, Rob.

As for his current job, he was responsible for the Marketing of the U.S. Chamber of Commerce publication *Nations Business*. He was also in charge of managing the advertising space Sales Executives for the magazine.

How strange after all these years we were now working in the same town and in the same building complex. I would never have predicted this possibility. I was excited to be a working professional and to be having a business lunch with my dad.

As I made my way through the office, a few fellow sales guys asked if I wanted to grab a quick lunch with them. We were in the high-tech computer systems sales profession and we often were on GO with little time for a lunch. As I grabbed my suit coat and started putting it on while walking out, I announced, "Not today, boys. I'm off to have a real lunch with my dad!"

It took just a few minutes to make my way through the joining maze of connecting hallways and up the stairs to the entrance of Diamond Jim's. The restaurant was decorated to look like an old western saloon. The entrance had swinging doors, like an old west bar. Whenever I pushed through those doors I felt like I should draw my six-shooters ready for a gun fight.

I walked in and looked around the dimly lit room for my dad and spotted him in a booth. He glanced up but quickly looked back at his menu. He didn't recognize me!

I was wearing a three-piece blue suit, white starched button-down shirt, with a bright red and blue club tie. My dad was not used to seeing me dressed this way. No ratty blue jeans and T-shirt, my typical college attire. I was now dressed like him. I approached the table and declared, "Hi, Dad! Ready for our first business lunch?" He quickly looked up, almost startled. He actually took a double take. "*Wow!* Look at my little boy now all dressed for success." Then he stood up and shook my hand.

Even our handshake was different on this day, strong and firm. We were now two businessmen meeting for lunch. Our father/son relationship would forever be changed. I am sure there is a moment in all parents' lives when their children go through this "change of life," from dependent kid to adulthood. My dad had dealt with businessmen most of his working life. Everyone dressed the same— suit and tie. And even though I was becoming one of them, up until now his vision was still of me as a "kid."

He stared at me for a few minutes and just shook his head. My dad was in his late forties and very handsome. Many people thought he looked like Robert Culp; today they would say he resembled George Clooney. My dad also looked very young. For many years, people asked if he was my older brother. I was not a fan of the question because it made me feel . . . old. He, on the other hand, loved the question.

This first lunch together had a strange feel to it, not at all uncomfortable, just different. Years later at another Friday lunch, we talked about this first lunch date. Dad explained to me that he had felt overcome with pride and a little bit of disbelief. He was amazed that we were able to have such a lunch date and that I was doing so well, especially considering what I went through in childhood.

2

Struggling to Live

As a young boy I was afflicted with a severe form of asthma (infectious asthma). It developed when I was four years old and went from bad to worse. Back in the 1960s, treating asthma was more art than science. It was not uncommon for kids to die from it. Many of the medical advancements that have been made in the United States from the 1960s to today are unimaginable to me. We went from launching monkeys into space in 1961 to having a man walking on the moon in 1969. Medical advancement was on a similar fast track.

Asthma back in the 1960s was like breast cancer—often a death sentence. Today, you seldom hear of a person in our country dying from asthma. (And if it is detected early, the five-year survival rate for breast cancer is now 98 percent.)

When I got a simple cold, it progressed to pneumonia quickly. Then it would trigger the asthmatic complication, and I struggled to breathe. The bronchial tubes in my lungs would constrict and close. I wheezed—the noise of air trying to squeeze through the inflamed passageways to replenish much needed oxygen. The lack of oxygen would cause many children with asthma to simply die from suffocation. Successful treatment in those days meant being hospitalized for five to ten days. When I had an asthma attack, I would be rushed to St. Joseph Hospital in Ann Arbor, Michigan, where I was finally able to breathe freely again with the aid of an oxygen mask.

Along with the oxygen mask the nurse would have to insert a long needle into my arm to administer a concoction of strong antibiotics. The worst part was always the poking and re-poking that occurred until she could find a suitable vein to insert the four-inch needle. As if this fine experience wasn't bad enough, I had to be quarantined because my immune system was shut down. Being alone, in a strange hospital room with tubes running out of my arm was unreal. Being hospitalized is an unpleasant experience for an adult. For a young child, sheer horror.

Even when I was not sick, sometimes I would have asthma attacks for no apparent reason. I would just start wheezing, coughing, and gasping for air. Not a great family moment. My mom and dad would call a neighbor to watch my brother and sister, then rush me off to the hospital. Back in those days, it was rare to call an ambulance since they were only located at the hospital themselves; it would have taken over an hour for an ambulance to make this roundtrip. As a result, my dad developed pretty good Indianapolis 500 racing skills. We made this trip about five or six times a year.

Now that I am a parent, I realize how terrifying my asthma attacks must have been for my parents. I am sure they wondered whether I would survive each attack.

In the third grade I was sick so often, I had to be homeschooled for most of the school year. I could not go out and play at all. I stayed inside and away from anybody who sneezed. This was the worst year of my life. My doctors, Drs. Preuss and Lovel, were not encouraged by my lack of progress and began working with researchers at the University of Michigan Hospital in Ann Arbor on my case. The doctors suggested putting me on a new, experimental drug. They were cautious but hopeful. My parents even discussed the idea with me before deciding to try it. I had one response: "I'm sick and tired of being sick and stuck in the house."

The decision was made. My parents signed the necessary papers and then waited for me to get sick again. It did not take long. After they fiddled with the dosage, the "modern" medicine was put to work—and work it did. Although I still got sick, the medicine could be administered at home and the recovery was now just a few days. Breathing was easier. I had to make only a few more visits to the hospital after receiving this new drug treatment.

I still had asthma attacks and they usually came on at night, but the treatment at home was less traumatic than being rushed to the emergency room. My mom had studied nursing at the University of Michigan, so she was well equipped to help administer the necessary shots to save my life. If I was in bed when I had an attack, she would always hear me and spring into action. She would run to the kitchen, boil some water to sterilize the needle, fill the syringe with medicine, and then quickly plunge the needle into my arm as I was gasping to breathe. Within just a few minutes my bronchial tubes would begin to open and I would be able to breathe normally again.

The drug that probably saved my life was prednisone. It is still used today for treating asthma along with many other medical problems. It was this anti-inflammatory drug that allowed me to finally breathe.

I know it was very painful for my dad to watch me endure so much during all those years. Now after all those trips to the hospital, and witnessing the late-night medical heroics, here we were having lunch together, father and son—and healthy.

My mom, Marian, as a nursing student at the
University of Michigan in 1946.

3

The Seeds of an Entrepreneurial Quest

"My father gave me the greatest gift anyone could give another person. He believed in me."

—Jimmy Valvano (1946-1993),
basketball coach of North Carolina State

At Diamond Jim's all the waitresses dressed like they were dance hall girls from the Wild West: low-cut white blouses with a lot of lace, many-layered red and black short skirts that flared out, garter belts for all the world to see. They were clearly catering to businessmen from the massive office building population. It was a strange contrast—all the customers wore suits and ties and the waitresses looked like they just traveled in time from 1875 to take our lunch orders. My dad and I both ordered steak sandwiches with fries. Neither of us were health-conscious guys. Besides, Diamond Jim's had the best steak sandwich in town.

Our conversation started with the typical small talk. "How's the job going? What do you think about the computer business?" However, we quickly moved onto my dad's favorite topic, becoming an entrepreneur. My dad loved to talk about being an entrepreneur and had high hopes that I would eventually make the break from corporate America and start a business of my own. It did not surprise me then that as the piping hot sandwiches arrived, Dad opened with: "How ironic our first lunch starts on a cold snowy day. Do you remember how your entrepreneurial quest first started?"

I replied, "Of course, the snow-covered sidewalks of Harding and Hartsough Streets in Plymouth. Does the neighborhood still have a kid shoveling the sidewalks?"

He continued, "No, but I sure wish we had an enterprising Tommy Gotshall."

I said, "Well it starts with a dad like you who is willing to show the way and encourage."

I remembered well how my entrepreneurial quest started fourteen years ago, the conversation my dad and I had about the mission. I even remember my first customer. Back when I was a ten-year-old, I was known to announce that I would someday play pro football. My brother would comment, "Tommy, I don't see you playing middle linebacker for the Green Bay Packers."

My dad would join the conversation: "True; however, he will probably be a millionaire someday." My brother, Rob, would laugh out loud, but my dad would stop him and say, "Really, you just wait and see." Money never starts an idea; it's the idea that starts the money to flow.

Growing up in the Midwest was like many areas of the United States, except one little thing—snow. Most everyone living in the South or West thinks we are nuts to put up with the cold and snow. And it is true that as soon as many people retire, they get the heck out and head south for the winter.

Yet, this weather has its upside too. The one advantage as kids was that we had "snow days" if it was determined by some top-secret governing body that snow was just too deep for normal bus and car transportation. On those blessed days, a snow day was declared— no school today. It was like going to Disneyworld. Today, school systems that deal with snow plan five or six of the dream days in the calendar. But back in my day, it was a big deal and a rare occurrence. No, the snow day czar was not quick to declare a snow day.

One December, when I was ten years old and in the fifth grade, we heard that a big storm was traveling fast out of the west and picking up steam. As the arctic cold would come down from Canada and meet this storm over Lake Michigan, it would pick up a ton of moisture and wallop us with snow.

As kids, we were not interested in the news, only sports and weather and only weather if a big storm was on its way. As bedtime approached, my brother and I would usually inquire about how the pro football playoffs were shaping up. I was a big Green Bay Packers fan, even living in Detroit, and I thought Vince Lombardi was the greatest football coach ever. The black and blue division was the best back then—the monsters of the Midwest. The Chicago Bears were also great. But on this night, my brother quickly turned the conversation from sports to the weather. "Dad, what's it looking like for tomorrow . . . much snow?" "Hard to tell; we will check the TV in the morning," was the reply.

The next morning was like all school mornings, my mom would wake up with the sound of the alarm clock. Then she and my dad would get up, followed by the oldest of the Gotshall kids, my sister, Kathy (she hated morning back then and still does). Then my brother, Rob, would stumble out, and finally I would rise. On this particular morning, my brother and I quickly turned on the TV. This was never allowed unless a snow day was looming.

As the TV was warming up, I opened the front door. Our outside storm door was six inches above the front porch. If the door cleared the snow, usually off to school. If it hit snow as it was opened, we had a chance. On this day I hit snow—two to three inches. So the total was probably eight or nine inches. We Gotshall boys took this measurement very seriously.

My mom was in the kitchen preparing breakfast, my dad pouring his first cup of coffee. As we watched the morning news anchor talk about the big storm that had hit the area, the banner along the bottom of the screen scrolled, listing the school closings in alphabetical order county by county, school district by district. Finally, it was up to Wayne County, where we attended Plymouth Community Schools. And then the best pre-Christmas present: "Plymouth Community School District, all area schools closed." A mass celebration broke out. My brother and I high-fived each other and ran into the kitchen to announce the fantastic news.

My sister immediately headed back to bed while my brother and I planned the "free day" events. As for my dad, his work didn't have snow days. This simply meant a long, slow drive into his office in downtown Detroit. For my mom, this meant kids in and out of the house all day covered in snow. My dad said something like, "Settle down; do something productive on your day off." Yeah, sure, we thought to ourselves.

My dad donned his suit and wingtips, pulled on his rubber boots over his shoes, put on a heavy topcoat, and headed out to clean off the car and slip and slide down the road. Meanwhile, my brother and I hurried to change into our play clothes, boots, big coats, scarves, hats, and gloves. We couldn't wait to get out to the snow with all the other boys in the neighborhood. And what a grand day we had that day—building snow forts, having snowball fights, even throwing an occasional snowball at the city trucks that were cleaning the streets. A great day indeed. That night after dinner, my dad and I were both sitting in the living room. I was watching *Gilligan's Island* or something like that, and he was reading the newspaper. After a while, he asked me, "What did you do today?"

I replied, "Goofed around."

He probed further. "What do you mean?"

So, I gave him the details about a ten-year-old's perfect day: the fort, snowball fights with our buddies next door, and so on.

He stopped reading, dropped the newspaper down, and said, "You missed an opportunity to earn some disposable income today."

Of course, I had no idea what he was talking about and he knew it as well. I would later look back at this day as the first of many conversations with my dad that were essentially coaching sessions. At a young age, and throughout my life, he was preparing me to make my own way in this world. Maybe he saw something in me that sparked an entrepreneurial chord in him. Maybe it was because I had been so sick with asthma much of my childhood. After all, he knew I wasn't going to play football for the Packers and he declared I was going to be a millionaire. He needed to do his part and push me along, beginning at age ten. None of this occurred to me at the time. I only thought, "Why is he jamming me and not Kathy or Rob?" Damn, I was trapped. I asked him what he was talking about and so started my education.

He uttered the words "Cash is king" and then explained: "If you have money, you don't have to depend on anybody else. You don't have to hope the government, your parents, friends, or anyone will 'Help you out.' Disposable income is money you have earned and you can dispose of, or spend, anyway you want. Nobody can tell you what to do with it. The more you have, the better. Cash is king . . . of the hill. Currently, your parents are providing you with food, shelter, clothes, salvation, etc. So 100 percent of what you earn, you decide just how to spend it. Today, if you want to go to the candy store and buy a pop and candy bar, you have to ask or depend on your parents to provide you with the capital (cash) for the transaction. If you want to go to the movies on Saturday, again you have to hope they will give you the money. If you saved a lot, however, you could buy what you want; you could even go out and purchase the type of bike you want, not waiting for your brother's hand-me-downs."

This disposable income thing made sense to me; it really sounded great. I quickly asked, "So what opportunity was lost and how could I have earned some money today?" My dad told me that I could have charged people for shoveling their snow. He said it took him half an hour just to get out of our driveway this morning because of all the snow. Although my brother and I were responsible for shoveling our snow for no payment, my dad explained that not every family has a Rob and Tommy to do the labor. Wow! He was right; I knew the neighborhood and so many houses didn't have "young labor." He said, "I bet some of our neighbors would gladly hire you to shovel their snow." As much sense as this made, the opportunity had been lost. The next day, back to the coal mines—school. However, this was the winter of 1966 and luck was on my side. All entrepreneurs need some luck.

Two weeks later, we heard that another big storm was on its way. My mom described it as a blinger. As we prepared for bed, we were already getting hammered with snow. My brother and I popped out of bed the next morning, I turned on the TV, and he opened the front door. Snow everywhere, maybe one foot. Sure enough, the newscaster announced that a major storm was again hitting the Midwest and that all public and private schools in the tri-county area would be closed today. Great joy filled the Gotshall house. My brother and I danced around, whooping it up. My sister, Kathy, told us we were idiots and returned to bed.

At breakfast, my dad uttered, "Oh to be a school kid again." He knew the drive ahead of him would probably take two or three hours instead of the normal hour.

After breakfast, Rob was lounging around in his pajamas, not doing much of anything. I went to my room and when I emerged, I was dressed and ready for action. My dad's message after the last snowstorm was crystal clear in my mind and I was on a mission. I finished getting ready for work—boots, heavy coat, gloves, and hat. My mom asked, "What's the hurry?" Rob said, "What's up?" I replied, "I'm now a working man and I'm off to earn a living."

My brother chuckled and my mom said, "Sure Tommy, go and have a fun day, see you at lunchtime."

I was surprised at their response but concluded neither of them knew about disposable income and the great opportunity that awaited just outside the door. I grabbed our best snow shovel, hoisted it over my shoulder, and off I went. The snow seemed much deeper than it looked. All the better, I figured. Down the street and up to the first door I went, rang the doorbell . . . nobody answered. Next house, same result. Had my dad sent me on a wild goose chase? Was there really an opportunity here? Finally, at the third house, someone answered. I asked, "Do you need your walks shoveled?" "No thanks," and the door closed. Never mind; I was still determined to fulfill my mission. I looked up and down the streets; nobody was out—no cars and no people. Was it too early? Except for my sister, Kathy, we were all up. My dad had already left for work. I forged on.

The next house belonged to Mr. Simmons. All of us kids thought he was a crazy Scotsman; he even had an accent. Still, up to the door I went, rang the bell, out he came. He looked like he was seven feet tall. He had dust brooms for eyebrows and his hair stuck out in various directions. We all stayed away from him, because he seemed a little strange and they didn't have any kids. "Hello, Tommy. What can I do for you?" I replied, "Mr. Simmons, I'm out earning money and I wonder if I can shovel the snow off your walks."

"Sure, my boy, and how about the driveway as well."

I had closed my first transaction. He went on: "How much?" I froze. I had never thought about an amount. During all the years of doing labor at our house, my dad always said, "Your payment is dinner tonight." I had no idea what the "value of shoveling" for money equation should be. I asked, "What do you think?" and he replied, "How about four bits?"

I can remember this like it was yesterday. The problem was I had no idea what four bits amounted to. I knew it must be money, so I agreed. This was a mistake. I should have clarified the amount, but I was just excited to have my first customer.

So I began the job. I was experienced at snow shoveling; it wasn't usually too hard, especially with my brother working alongside me.

However, now I was on my own. And the snow was probably over a foot deep. After pushing and digging for about an hour, I finally finished. I returned to the front door, sweat rolling down my face, my hair matted under my wool stocking cap. As I rang the doorbell, I pulled off my hat; steam was billowing off my head as Mr. Simmons answered the door. I am sure he was amused with how I looked. Still, most everyone respects hard work, especially work done for them. He came out and inspected the job.

"My boy, ya sure did a fine job," he said. Then he dug his hand into his pocket and pulled out two quarters. Now I realized—four bits were just two quarters. Bad deal, I figured, but I tried not to show my disappointment. I asked, "Is there anything else I can do for you?" "Nope, that will be fine," he said. I turned and started heading down his clean sidewalk but turned when he called out, "Come back, Tommy." I figured he had noticed a patch of snow I might have missed. Instead, Mr. Simmons taught me something that cold winter morning. "Tommy, do you think you deserve more than four bits for the job?" he questioned me.

I had been taught to respect my elders, but I was up to the task. "Well, Mr. Simmons," I explained, "I didn't realize how deep the snow was or just how long the job would take." But for some crazy reason, I also said, "A deal is a deal." I am sure he was amused by my philosophizing. He replied, "Many people will take advantage of you in life. You must state your worth and hold your ground." Then that crazy Scotsman pulled out his wallet, which looked about the size of a loaf of bread, and said the job was worth three dollars and here it is. He pulled three fresh, crisp one-dollar bills out of his wallet and handed them to me. He went on to say, "And the four bits is your tip for doing an extra good job." I was in disbelief—$3.50 could buy a lot in those days. I didn't know just what to say but I am sure my shocked expression was priceless.

Still, this man was not done. He said, "Tommy, anytime it snows, please come by and shovel my walks and driveway. I will pay you the same." My first regular customer. Reoccurring revenue—things fortune are made of.

I almost ran to my next house, I was so pumped up. My dad was the smartest man in the world, I thought. My profit—$3.50—was the most/only money I had ever earned in my life and I could spend it on anything I wanted. Ahhhhh, disposable income.

Mrs. Wilson was next. I marched up to her door, and out she came. I now had such confidence. "Mrs. Wilson," I said, "would you like me to shovel your walks and driveway today?" "Sure," she replied. Before she could say another word, I said. "I charge three dollars plus four bits for the work." She smiled, knowing I had been across the street doing Mr. Simmons's walks. At the conclusion of the job, she too asked to become a regular customer. After another two jobs, I made my way home for tomato soup and grilled cheese, my favorite winter lunch. My brother was still in his pajamas reading comic books. I saw my mom, and she inquired, "Have you been at the Beaver's house?" (No kidding, the name of my buddy across the street was Brian Beaver.)

I explained, "No, I was out doing man's work and earning disposable income." Rob looked up from the *Archie's* comic book and said, "Huh?" My mom replied, "How nice." Rob was still staring at me. I started telling my stories from the road, beginning with Mr. Simmons. Rob interrupted, "Not that cheap, crazy Scotsman?" I refuted, "Mr. Simmons is a fine man and now a regular customer of mine." I went on to tell the entire story. My brother was in disbelief. He kept saying, "$3.50?"

My mom also was staring at me in astonishment. "What possessed you to go and give this a try?" she asked. Mom was very protective of me because of all those years of dealing with asthma and endless hospitalizations. I know thoughts of doctors, hospitals, and experimental drugs raced through her mind as she pictured me shoveling piles of snow.

I did not tell my mom what really initiated my desire to start this business, about the conversation with my dad on the last snow day. I knew she would be mad at him. *Bob, sending Tommy out in the cold, shoveling snow all day! He could catch a cold and end up in the hospital again.* My dad, however, saw something in me that told him this was the type of guidance he needed to be giving me. More on that later.

So finally my brother asked, "Just how much did you make?" I pulled out a wad of cash, huge to me, and proceeded to count my money—one, two, three . . . The total was $17.27. My brother fell off the couch and my mom just continued to stare at me. For the first time, I felt like king. Lunch never tasted better, the three of us chatting away. Finally, my sister joined in, asking, "What's all the noise?" Rob said, "T's rich! Look at all the cash he has!" That afternoon, back out I went and did five more jobs.

That night the talk at the dinner table was about me, not about being sick as usual, but about me working and making money. So much of my life up until this point, I was out of the loop. This night it was different. My dad just beamed at my stories from the road. I know my mom was still concerned, wondering if I was going to get sick again.

My sister and brother looked at me very differently too. Not as their little sick kid brother, but as someone else. When I got up from the dinner table that night, I will never forget this, my sister, Kathy, asked, "Did you get taller today or grow or what?" That day I earned $36, and I grew one foot.

My education for the day had not concluded. Later my dad found me in my room, cash spread out on my bed and me working on a model car. He told me he was proud of me. Also he said that cash is great, but it is just a by-product of planning and hard work. Then he asked, "What else did you learn about your experience?" I thought real hard. The snow resulted in income. I was sore, I was tired, I had learned how to make change? I was not sure what he was asking for, so he explained: "Most people don't see opportunity, make a plan, and then follow through with it. The execution of the plan seldom takes place, because of distractions, lack of persistence, or just losing faith."

He asked me why after three rejections I continued and went to Mr. Simmons's house. I thought about this and replied, "The reason I pushed on was because I wanted to make some money and I saw all the snow covering our neighbors' sidewalks. So I figured sooner or later someone would hire me and pay me for the job." My dad told me I had wisdom beyond my years. Somehow I already knew the simple formula for success:

Opportunity and need + solution with value at a fair price = results and income.

I told him I was hired by six of my ten customers to shovel after every snowfall. He said, "Did you ask the other four if they would like you to return on other snow days?" I had not. He replied, "If you don't ask, how would you know if they were interested or not?" Another lesson: Sell by simply asking for the business. Inform prospective customers that a service is available. I could have said, "Mrs. Johnson, if you would like me to come and shovel anytime it snows, I would be happy to put you on my route of regular customer and you will always have a clear walk and drive." That winter I developed a list of seventeen regular customers. I adjusted my fee up and down if the snow was greater than eight inches or less than two. My dad developed a flyer with my home phone number and I put it in all of the mailboxes in the neighborhood. I made $450 that first winter.

The next spring, my dad and I went to downtown Plymouth and opened a savings account at the National Bank of Detroit (NBD). Dad told me I could spend the disposable income any way I wanted. However, he said, I should "enjoy" some of it and save the rest. He explained that saving and accumulating money was key to becoming wealthy and independent.

Years later I joked with him about this. I said, "First you convince me to go out and start a business so I could have cash to spend any way I wanted. Then you trick me into saving most of it so someday I could be rich. When do I get to enjoy it and spend it?" I asked.

But as with so many things, my dad was correct about this. I learned that with money, you have leverage. With leverage, you can create a business or buy a business and continue the cycle of wealth.

When I graduated from Plymouth Salem High School, I had saved more than $6,500 from my snow shoveling and lawn maintenance business along with other jobs I held in high school. Real money back then for an eighteen-year-old.

4

Blue Jeans and Pizza

"A father is more important than a hundred schoolmasters."

—George Herbert,
(1593-1633) English writer

That first lunch with my dad lasted two hours. The transformation that occurred during that time was very real. We started our lunch talking about our relationship when I was a young boy and covered many years. As we finished, I said, "We have to do this again, soon." This was the type of thing people say all the time and somehow never follow through with. Months turn into years and years pass way too fast. But on the end of that first lunch date, my dad said, "Great, and I have an assignment for you." My reply was, "Are you kidding?" "Nope," he said. "You are to research your two favorite things—blue jeans and pizza. Next Friday, same place, same time, and let's talk inventions." We stood and he took one last look at me, up and down, and said, "Yes, indeed, I think I would buy a computer system from you." And he was off.

Walking back to my office, I was thinking, I have already graduated from college. Why am I doing research and for my dad of all people? During all my years in high school, we seldom discussed academic material. Although I was not sure what this was all about,

I did my research; I would be ready. Remember, this was pre-Google and Bing. In fact, in 1983, no one had a home computer. Luckily, I was employed at a computer company and could get my hands on information.

I was excited when Friday finally rolled around again. I had my notes prepared with endless facts. This time I called Dad's office and talked with his secretary of fifteen years, Marsha. "Hi-ya, Tommy," she said. "I understand you and Pop-so are going back to Diamond Jim's for lunch?" She went on, "Okay but don't keep him two hours this time. As always, I'll make sure he's off the phone and on time."

As I left the office, the receptionist, Lynn, said, "Lunch again with your dad? What a great thing to do."

I got to Diamond Jim's first and found a table. Shortly after, in comes my dad. He seemed to know most everyone in the place. "Hey Bobby G., join us for a quick one," somebody shouted out. "No can do; I'm with my youngest son today." As my dad made his way over, a couple of well-dressed men followed. My dad introduced me and I stood to shake their hands. I looked over at my dad and saw that he was actually beaming. Both Norm and Mike said, "How cool, having a business lunch with your son." They stayed on chatting for just a few minutes and then departed.

After that, my dad and I had some small talk about sports, the weather, and family. Then he jumped right in with his favorite topic: "Do you remember when you returned from your snow-shoveling duties one Saturday and you commented that there must be an easier way to remove all that snow faster?"

"Yeah, I think I said it many times." As I recalled this event, the memory of the snow removal device came rushing back. "We blew that opportunity, didn't we?"

My dad replied, "Yes, we sure did, and you must learn from those lost and missed opportunities."

What happened was that after a long day of shoveling one Saturday, I came home complaining of the manual labor required for the job. Although I loved the entrepreneurial experience and especially the money, shoveling was hard manual work. When the snow was light and fluffy, it was great. I could finish a job like Mr. Simmons's in thirty minutes. However, if it was warmer than 25 degrees, the snow would be heavy and wet. The same job would require more muscle and time.

Although my dad was now in sales and marketing, he was an artist and engineer at heart. He attended college at the Lawrence Institute of Technology as an engineering major. He didn't finish because he met my mom, Marian Worden, fell in love, and got married within nine months and then needed to support his family. Those were different times and all of the servicemen from WWII were coming home and getting married—fast. Plus, many of them started families right away, hence the beginning of the Baby Boom. My dad was not in the war, because he had a medical condition that deemed him unfit for service; he was classified as 4 F. This condition was a result of a mishap during his birth that may be attributable to an incompetent midwife. During the birth, his right arm and shoulder were both broken in a number of places. When he was an infant, doctors tried repeatedly to break and reset his arm to correct the problem, but they were ultimately unsuccessful. As a result, my dad learned how to be left-handed.

Whenever I saw my dad without a shirt, I was always amazed at the scars running from his forearm up to his shoulder area. His right arm was also abnormally thin. Dad never really talked much about the scars or the problems with his arm. He only said, "It was the hand I was dealt, so I just ignored any crap I got and simply learned how to be a lefty." My dad was the most positive person on the planet. Period. There was never talk of blaming the midwife or all the doctors who tried to fix his arm. He felt grateful for their efforts and persistence!

That day, we talked about the need to remove snow faster and better. Dad had a sketch pad always handy, so he pulled it out and asked me to describe shoveling. I remember standing up in our living room and demonstrating the shoveling motion. Imaginary shovel, my hands low, push forward and throw to the left. Repeat and repeat. He asked, "What's the hardest part?" I told him the lifting and throwing to the side. Anyone who has shoveled knows what I am talking about.

This sets him in motion: "What if we design a device that looks like our lawnmower that you walk behind and push, and it throws the snow to the right or left?" "Really?" I said. "Great . . . but how?" As we are talking, my dad drew a push mower with a hood above the blades that ends as a funnel. The "snow thrower" was designed to push the snow up and into a blade-like device that fed the snow into a chute and funneled it by throwing it left or right depending on how the operator set the funnel. No kidding, my dad drew and designed the first snow blower. The Toro snow blower of today could have been the Gotshall thrower. The company could have been Gotshall Enterprises.

One big reason this did not happen was because the sketch and design of this invention stayed on my dad's pad with all the notes. We talked about it many times, especially whenever I returned from my shoveling duties. Unfortunately, that is where the idea stopped and eventually died in a typical entrepreneur's dream and vision graveyard. We sort of laughed about it at lunch that day and talked about what could have been.

My dad then shifted the topic slightly, "Let's talk about a few men who didn't let their dreams die. Tell me about your research on blue jeans and pizza."

I retrieved my legal pad with my notes and told my dad that I researched the Levi Strauss Company and Domino's Pizza, headquartered in our first hometown, Ann Arbor Michigan.

First I tell him about Levi's history.

Here's a classic, Levi's. Levi Strauss went to San Francisco in 1853 to open a dry goods store. During the gold rush of the mid-1800s, prospectors would frequent his store. Some complained their pants were ripped to shreds because they were on their knees panning for gold all day.

Levi responded to this problem by taking a bolt of heavy canvas, originally used for making strong sails, and designing a product—the first pair of denim overalls—with the miners in mind. He also reinforced them with those famous pop rivets, which are still on some styles today. Word quickly spread and before long he was overwhelmed with miners looking to buy his "Levi" branded overalls.

Eventually, the dry goods business fell by the wayside and Levi Strauss began production of Levi's. No one is sure if the first to wear a pair of Levi's was a gold miner, or a cowboy, or a lumberjack, or a railroad worker. But it's clear the invention was made for people doing hard labor. As an entrepreneur, you must keep open to new ideas and ask yourself, How can I improve all aspects of what we are doing?

In 1930, the product was local to the West Coast working class. However, during the dude ranch craze of the 1930's, Easterners returned home with tales and examples of hard-wearing pants with rivets. And their popularity grew along the entire East Coast.

During WWII, only those working in the defense manufacturing industry were allowed to purchase Levi's. Then in the 1950s and 1960s, Levi's became popular with the youth subculture and the explosion was on.

The company is still owned by the descendants of Levi Strauss. Back in 1983, I could not find any financial information on the company because it was privately held. Today, the Levi company has more than over 22,000 employees, fifty plants, and offices in thirty-five countries. In 2010, revenue was $1.29 billion, with a fourth-quarter net profit of $67 million. Because the company is privately held, it is still difficult to get more detailed information.

I am sure Levi Strauss never envisioned that his first simple pair of "blue jeans" in the 1850s would become a major success. The same is true today: there are an endless amount of entrepreneurial opportunities just waiting to be discovered and launched into businesses—and some of these ideas will take off.

My dad listened patiently as I reported on my research and then said, "The very existence of Levi's today is because an individual walked into a dry goods store and told young Levi Strauss about a problem, ripped-out pant knees, and he took *action*."

Right place and right time. Pants had been around forever. The key to Levi's success was the thick canvas material, with rivets. The suggestion to use copper rivets to strengthen the pants came from Jacob Davis, who partnered with Levi Strauss. It was by word of mouth that his product sold and his company exploded.

After our "blue jeans" conversation, my dad wanted to talk about the rest of my research. "Now tell me about your essential food group, pizza," he said. I did my research on Domino's Pizza.

Tom Monaghan and his brother bought a pizza store in 1960 called DomiNick's for $75. They borrowed $500 for operating expenses and to open their first store. Their first purchase was a VW Bug. Their idea was to deliver pizzas to local University of Michigan and Eastern Michigan students. Although they had the pizza store for walk-in business, they knew that college kids were busy studying or doing whatever and often did not or could not get to their store. The Monaghans did not invent the pizza, but they did invent home—or dorm—delivery. Plus, their key slogan was FAST, FAST, FAST.

In fact, they guaranteed delivery in thirty minutes or the pizza was *free*. When college kids decide they want a pizza, they want it *now*—and Tom and his brother knew this. Almost overnight, their business took off. It actually took off too fast. They quickly opened two more stores with little capital. After a while, Tom's brother decided he did not want to be in the pizza business anymore. His buyout was the VW BUG.

Tom Monaghan was now in the business alone, but he felt his vision was unstoppable. The growth of Domino's was explosive—so much so that the company went bankrupt not once, but three times in the early years. The primary reason was cash flow. They were spending more on expansion than they were taking in. Poor cash flow management is the principal reason that businesses fail. But Tom Monaghan did not let even this stop him; he picked himself up off the mat again and again. He convinced a few very smart and lucky friends to loan him a small amount of money—$2,500. This got Domino's over the hump and rolling. In 1983, Domino's had hundreds of stores in the United States. Today Domino's has over 9,000 stores in sixty countries.

Tom Monaghan became a billionaire. He bought the Detroit Tigers and later sold them to another pizza billionaire, Mike Illitch. Tom eventually left Domino's to pursue his next passion—founding Ava Maria College in Florida. If you are an entrepreneur, always keep your eye on the mission and goals of your company. However, also be thinking of ways to change or improve the process or product.

My dad and I spent the rest of the lunch talking about the greatness some entrepreneurs achieve. He was not bitter about the lost opportunity with the snow blower device but advised me to learn from our missed project. All successful entrepreneurs keep at it. As we parted that Friday, he said, "Tom, keep your day job because you worked hard to get where you are today. However, always be thinking one step ahead of your current job. You were destined for greatness!"

5

Gotshall Maintenance

A wise son hearth his father's instruction.
—The Bible, Matthew 13:1

Lunch with Dad became a regular event. It was understood that each Friday we would get together at Diamond Jim's. My dad and I were expected at our normal booth. From time to time, friends of my dad would come by to say hello. But they would never join us. Everyone commented that it was grand we had this routine.

On one occasion we talked about my snow shoveling business again. One of the really great things about our lunches was that we shared our thoughts about events from so many years ago.

I reminded him of a conversation we had after my first winter season of shoveling. As winter turned to spring, my business was about to die, or so I thought. One evening in March, my dad asked, "What's next, my budding entrepreneur?" I asked what an entrepreneur was. He explained the definition as one who starts, organizes, manages, and assumes all the risks and rewards of a business or enterprise.

I replied, "Well, okay. I think my business opportunity is about to . . . die." He of course asked why I would think such a thing. "Well, it's late March," I said, "and my business depends on snow. And no snow means no business." I am actually thinking maybe my dad is not such a great business visionary, maybe not so bright. How could I make any money if there wasn't any snow to shovel?

But then he asked me, "Each spring what do you and Robby have to do at our house?"

Without hesitation, I knew exactly what he talking about. "Oh crap, the dreaded spring cleanup." Stuff everywhere—sticks, leaves, junk that has been covered all winter by the snow. Rob and I were assigned this messy task every year in early April.

My dad would get five or six large plastic bags for us. He would wake us up early on a Saturday morning on a day when it was usually still chilly. We were given gloves and our "orders" to go pick up everything in the yard. The dead debris was always wet and smelled of old dead moss. Rob, thinking it was funny, would often find a time when I was turned away and then grab a handful of soaking wet goop and pelt me with it on the side of my face. A rumble would ensue; I usually got the short end of the tussle. Neither of us liked this job, but we did not get a vote in the matter.

And shortly after our cleanup, usually late April or early May, the dormant grass would start to grow. Then the task of weekly mowing would start, not my favorite thing to do because of my asthma. However, the rule was I took every other week.

My dad said, "I wonder who takes care of that stuff for your customers." Just the sound of that "your customers" sounded great.

Since most of my regulars did not have anyone to shovel the snow, they probably would be interested in a spring cleanup service and maybe regular grass mowing as well.

Flyer # 2
Spring Cleanup Service
Removal of:
Leaves
Sticks/branches
General yard debris
Lawn mowing also available.

Call Tommy Gotshall
453-1234

My career was not over, just beginning.

I put a flyer in over fifty house mailboxes. One week later, my dad suggested I go around and "ask for the business." He said to be very polite and to take a pad of paper and build my list of jobs and schedule them with dates.

I got more business than I could handle. I had to enlist the help of my brother and Brian Beaver for the spring cleanup jobs. This cut into some of my profits; however, with their help I was able to do three times the number of jobs I could do on my own and make a lot more money overall. These were my very first employees and during this experience I learned how to delegate responsibilities. I also learned the financial power of leverage.

From the conversation on the snow day in December, I started Gotshall Maintenance. It was a full-service business: snow shoveling, spring cleanup, mowing, and fall leaf removal.

6

Just a Normal Kid

"Small boys become big men through the influence of big men who care about small boys."

—Anonymous

As weeks turned into months, lunch with my dad continued. It was now firmly entrenched into both of our schedules. Also, no holds barred—we discussed everything. We were now like two old college buddies uncovering all the details of our past together. Not only was it exhilarating; it was revealing.

On one particular Friday, we were reviewing vacations and other outings.

Photo of my dad and me on camping trip, 1963

When I was growing up, my parents felt we should get involved in many activities—sports, music, and scouts. One spring when the scouts had their annual camping trip, I was sick and could not go. Spring was my bad season. As everything began to blossom in Michigan, the "bad" stuff would come out; pollen, weeds, dust and mold. It was a cycle. First the allergies would kick into gear, then a cold and soon pneumonia. And then back to the hospital. I was very mad I had to miss the big camping trip.

In the fall, as the frost came, all the pollen and ragweed would die. This was my best season for health. My dad knew I was still disappointed that I had missed out on that camping trip. After I had been feeling better for a while, he came home one Friday and announced that the Gotshall boys were going camping. There was one condition: I had to wear my Boy Scout uniform, hat and all.

I was thrilled. Plus, I knew my dad was not a camping-type guy. Camping to my dad was not staying at a five-star hotel, but at one with only four stars. But he bought a tent and sleeping bags, and off we went. We went canoeing on the Au Sable River and camped for three days. I remember that it was really cold but that my brother and I had a great time. Rob said it was a lot more fun than the scouting trip the previous spring.

Many years later my dad told me that he was never colder in his life than on that camping trip. Sleeping on the ground in a tent was not his idea of a vacation. However, seeing his boys have such a great time canoeing, fishing, and cooking outdoors made the experience well worth the whole deal.

In turn, I told my dad the camping trip had an impact on me that would last a lifetime. Dad was not an emotional type of guy. Men were expected to be the strong, silent type back in his day. Yet when I told him over lunch how profoundly the Gotshall camping trip affected me, I saw my dad shed a tear for the first time in my life. The trip had helped me realize that I could be a normal kid. Even with asthma, I could do many things other kids could do. Being normal was all I wanted.

The emotionally positive impact this realization had on me changed my life and gave me confidence for the first time.

7

Moving On

I worked Gotshall Maintenance for five years and made $3,500. When I started high school, I got involved in sports and other activities and had less and less time for taking care of my customers. I ended up migrating most of them to a few kids in the neighborhood. However, I retained a few key accounts, like Mr. Simmons. During high school I held various part-time jobs and was able to save another $3,000, for a total of $6,500. The best part of this was that I always had money for whatever I wanted.

My dad told me one day: "Confidence and knowledge come from experience." Over those five years with my maintenance company, I grew as a person and as an entrepreneur. Many children with an illness struggle with a feeling of not fitting in and dread. Learning how to fit in and being part of activities are critical lessons and development in childhood. For kids who are unable to participate, this can be a tough time. I was lucky to avoid this fate. My self-worth went from low to very high because of my successful entrepreneurial experiences.

I learned to communicate with adults when they were the customers. Mr. Simmons loved to talk to me about money and the importance of being frugal, saving, and the options it gives. Even today, I still draw on the lessons I learned from my days developing and running my snow and lawn business, lessons that served me in running a multi-million dollar computer integration business. From that first business, I learned how to communicate, present, and sell. I also learned the importance of organization and scheduling. Most important, I realized if you provided more service than expected, you will receive more opportunity. Most businesses provide only what is expected and nothing more. Because I always made a point to do a little extra work, my contracts would expand and my reputation became top notch.

All these things resulted in more business and thereby more income.

8

The Neighborhood

I remember one particular Friday lunch with Dad. It was a hot, humid summer day in Michigan. Even though the buildings were all air-conditioned, I was sweating through my dress shirt and my tie was sticking to it. As I entered Diamond Jim's for lunch, I saw that the place was packed and noisy. The Detroit Tigers were on the bar TVs and most of the patrons were watching and talking above the game.

As always, my dad looked cool when I found him sitting in our booth. As I approached, he stood up and greeted me in his manner with a big smile and firm handshake. "Hi ya, T. Looks like the Tigers are having their way with the Cleveland Indians today; it's 5-0 in the second inning already."

I replied, "Yes, it's great to see our team doing well."

My dad must have been thinking about summers around our neighborhood because he asked me a question before we ordered. "As you were growing up, I knew a lot about some things that were going on in your life—the maintenance business, your neighborhood pals—but what other types of things were going on? Tell me about the dynamics of the neighborhood."

I flashed back in time as a flood of memories rushed to mind. The summer uniform was blue jeans and a T-shirt with the name of some sports team on it. Tennis shoes were worn every day and were usually destroyed by the end of summer.

I started out:

> As I turned twelve, thirteen, then fourteen, my asthma improved. However, it was always looming but under control. I could now play the neighborhood sports with the other kids. Spring was basketball, summer was baseball, and fall was football. When we played a pickup game in the neighborhood, Rob was usually a captain and would pick me, but usually late in the team selection process. They called me Wheeze. It wasn't bullying though; everybody had a descriptive nickname. Plus I did still wheeze a bit because of my asthma. My buddy Brian was a little heavy so they called him Donut. His brother Greg was tall and skinny; he was Slim. Jamie Lent was the oldest kid, so we called him Gramps. Rob was fast! He was Wheels. As kids, we always did a lot of teasing. Some in fun, some not. But when anybody would call me out during a local baseball game: "Hey Wheeze, nice strikeout . . . loser," Brian Beaver, my buddy, would pipe in: "Maybe he sucks at baseball, but he's the richest kid in the neighborhood and probably the whole world."
>
> I didn't have to say much to defend myself; kids would look to Rob and he would say, "Sorry to agree with you Donut, but it's true." After all, both Rob and Brian had been employed by me and were well aware of the amount of money I was making working in the snow shoveling, spring cleanup, and lawn business.
>
> Brian never had cash, but I always did. He was my pal, so when we would go up to Rengert's market on the corner, I would treat him sometimes to a pop

and candy. I discovered the enjoyment you get from spreading the "wealth." Just look at Bill Gates and Warren Buffett. They give millions away to help others. It is all relative. When I treated Brian to a pop and candy bar as kids, it was big time.

I told my dad that the neighborhood dynamics taught all of us a lot about getting along and how to organize events, like sports. A pecking order was always established, and without parents and adult supervision, we figured things out.

Today, most kids are over-supervised, over-managed, and over-controlled. The days of a group of neighborhood kids picking up any type of sporting event (or anything) are long gone. It is too bad because we all grew from these experiences.

As we finished lunch, I asked my dad why he thought I continued with that first business and was so driven at such a young age to excel in the business world.

He told me he thought I loved the cash, but more than that, I excelled at creating this local business. I made a name for myself and was proud of overcoming the challenges as a sick kid. One benefit of going through all those experiences of being sick was that when I was not sick anymore, it felt like a gift; I cherished being and feeling well. Anyone who goes through an extended illness appreciates when they simple feel better. I told my dad that maybe he was right. I just remember the feeling that running my own business gave me. I felt in control of the situation. And I loved having my own disposable income.

9

High School

One Friday we had lunch and it was 70 degrees out, a sunny and perfect fall day. Fall meant back to school for all the kids and football season. I remember all the phases of going back to school. In middle school, most kids are still under the control of their parents. However, in high school, the rules change. I remember this was the period when I had more decisions to make on my own.

At this particular lunch, we talked about these changes and my high school experience. As always, my dad openly probed, "As you were going from Junior High East to Plymouth Salem High School, what were you feeling?"

I was the youngest of the Gotshall kids and so was heavily influenced by the path that my sister, Kathy, and brother, Rob, had paved. My sister was class vice president and was in the marching band. My brother was class president and an all-state swimmer. My goal was to do all of these things: class president, swimmer, and marching band. Sort of a strange combination, but like many kid brothers, I idolized my older siblings.

On top of all that, my dad felt I should work at different jobs in and around Plymouth. He told me, "Son, these are the formative years. The more experiences you have, the more prepared you will be later in life for your entrepreneurial quest." Sitting around watching TV and goofing off were not options for us.

During lunch, I told my dad, "When I think about all the jobs I had, you were right; at a young age I learned a lot about business, hard work, and selling."

All of my various jobs gave me important insight and helped me develop skills. For a time, I worked at a farm just outside Plymouth, Brinks Farm. I was hired to bale hay for $2 an hour. I was the grunt. I stood on the flatbed truck and as the baler spit out a bale of hay, I was to grab it and stack it. When the flatbed was full, the driver would pull into the barn and I was to throw the bales up into the rafters.

This was summer in Michigan, and the temperature in the barn was around 110 degrees. Because of my lingering asthma and allergies, I paid for this outdoor experience—each night my nose would be all stuffed up, my eyes would turn red, and my breathing would become labored. Plus, I would be dead tired. My mom would fill a pan with water and bring it to a boil; then she'd have me stand above the pan with a towel over my head and breathe in the steam in an attempt to clear my nose and open my bronchial tubes. It helped but was not a total cure.

Working at the farm was only short term. I also worked at a grocery store as a stock boy.

My best job was working for Fred Hill. He owned John Smith's Clothing, a local men's clothing store. It was 1971, before massive malls and the Internet. Almost every man and young boy in town purchased their clothing at John Smith's Clothing.

Back then, my dad always told me to use every job as a learning opportunity. He said, "Fred Hill is a professional businessman and one of the best salesmen I have seen in action. Ask questions and listen." (That is, open probe and shut up.) My dad reminded me that I could learn many valuable things from Fred, so I should watch and listen carefully. After I was hired, I asked Mr. Hill many questions: How do you pick which clothes to carry? When do you buy your stock? How do you make money?

His department store was in downtown Plymouth. The main level featured a men's department with suits, accessories, and casual wear. The teens' and kids' cloths were downstairs, along with the Boy Scout equipment.

I soon found out that my dad was right; Fred was the master salesman. Not only did he know every customer's name, he knew his wife's name and kids' names. As a customer entered the store, I would hear him sing out, "Hello Bill. How's Marge and the kids? What can we get you today? The new Polo blazers just came in— very sharp."

He also knew most everyone's size. And he would lead them, like a fish on a line, over to the fitting area, take a blazer from the rack, put it on the guy. "Oh my gosh! Cary Grant wouldn't look better; maybe you could be a model in your spare time." The hook was set. Then he would reveal just how much he knew about his customers: "How about those Lions, Tigers, Red Wings, Pistons, U of M, or MSU?" depending on the season and the customer's favorite teams and sport. Fred was a pro salesman and part of his job was knowing what was going on with all the teams.

He would say, "Can you believe that Michigan quarterback Ricky Leach? What a game he had against Wisconsin last week— passing for 288 yards." Usually he would talk about a specific play: "Third and fifteen, he passed to White for the first down and next for the win. Unreal!" Fred knew the correct sales conversations, usually sports, never politics or religion unless the customer was big on that sort of thing. He knew whether they were Republican or Democrat. Most Plymouth men were Republican and all went to the Catholic, Methodist, or Presbyterian Church on Sunday.

I never knew what religion Fred was, but he knew every customer's affiliation and he worked it. Fred would tell me, "The key to selling, don't make it look like selling. Most everyone doesn't want to be sold. If they feel like they are being handled, they will resist. Your job is to 'guide' them to the best possible outcome."

During the sales process, everyone wants to be in control, get a great deal, and have choices. As an entrepreneur, you will be selling all the time—everything from your idea, to prospective employees, to customers, to suppliers, and on and on.

One day, I watched Fred sell a man named Bill a blazer, two shirts, a tie, socks, and boxers then run his credit card for $385 and send him on his way. All of those items and I do not recall hearing Bill request any of it. I waited until the store was empty at closing time to ask about it:

"Fred, Bill James came in and never really said he needs a new blazer and all that other stuff. But he bought it and was so pleased. What's that all about?"

Fred would look at me as if studying me, a fifteen-year-old. Then he would say, "T.G. (he called every employee by their initials), Bill came in today because he wanted to buy something; he maybe didn't even know just what. My job is to 'advise' him of the latest fashion. I knew he has six suits already in his closet. I sold them all to him. Men are starting to wear blazers to work. He works for Ford Motor Company in the finance department where blazers with a tie along with a white shirt and dark pants are acceptable now. Men, just like women, feel good when they buy new clothes. Assume the sale before it happens. The flow of the conversation about The University of Michigan football game makes him feel at ease. He is a graduate of the U of M and knows the team and the coach, Bo Schembechler. I'm like an old college buddy." I replied, "But you hate the U of M. You went to OSU and everybody knows you love Woody Hayes, the coach of Ohio State."

He said "True, but I wouldn't say to a customer, 'I hate Michigan and I hope OSU kills them.' I keep it light. Some customers like to debate it; then I will usually say, 'I know it will be a great game with much drama and great plays.' Never challenge the customer. Always know about both teams and keep it light."

When someone would come in wearing the clothes they purchased at John Smith's, you would think the president walked in: "Wow, Sam, you look great. Are you losing weight, working out, headed to Florida or what? All you need is a sweater vest to kill that outfit. All the young housewives will chase you around the grocery store." Sure enough, Fred would sell two vests, a belt, and a sports shirt—brilliant.

My job at the store was stock and inventory control. The trucks would pull in the alley behind the store, open the door, and shove the boxes and crates to the lift gate. The drivers were always big, strong, and in a hurry. "Hey kid, get your clipboard," they'd say.

I would get the clipboard. Hughes Hatcher eight boxes shirts, four boxes belts, twelve boxes underwear, fifteen boxes socks. The driver and I would count them together and pile them up outside the door to the elevator room. Then, we would both sign the delivery sheet, and the truck would be off in a cloud of exhaust.

I would take all the boxes to the attic, check all the inventory, and fill out the paperwork. Then I would price each item according to the F.H. (Fred Hill) pricing list and place it on the storage shelves. Fred had a specific number of floor inventory items he wanted. White dress shirts—all sizes, blue, stripes, etc. I was also responsible for counting the inventory each night after closing, filling out the log of what needed to be replenished, and then restocking. The stock job was not hard, just boring. Because we were in the store around customers, the stock boys were required to wear dark pants, a white button-down shirt, and a tie. Fred wanted us to look professional. Usually after two to four months, Fred would let us work the downstairs kids/teens area. If you could handle Mrs. Jones buying Jimmy's clothes for second grade or Pete buying a sweater, he would move you up to the main floor for the big time, as Fred called it.

The profit margin for men's suits, sweaters, blazers, and accessories was the gold mine of the store. On one busy Saturday, I was working the downstairs when my "big break" finally came.

I was called up to the main floor. Upstairs, the place was nuts. Fred said, "Take Mr. Johnson, fast." Mr. Johnson was looking over topcoats. I went into F.H. mode: "Hello, Mr. Johnson (Tigers fan). Looking for a topcoat to wear to the Tigers' game? The Tigers' season is almost over, but the topcoats just arrived." I seemed to get his attention. He said, "I see Fred's a little busy—but if you could show me a forty-six long, that would be great." I did my best F.H. imitation that day, and I sold one topcoat, one sports shirt, and two pair of socks. Success.

What I took away from the clothing store business and Fred Hill has served me well over the years. All successful entrepreneurs are also salespeople. Bill Gates (the richest person in the world for many years) had to sell his first computer and idea. Billionaire Sam Walton was a hardware store owner and salesperson first. Selling is part of the arsenal of things everyone must master to be a successful entrepreneur. It pays to get some experience in this area along the way.

10

The Photo

During one late-summer lunch, my dad and I talked about pictures and how some parents take endless photos and some take none.

I start out: "Dad, do you regret not having a camera and taking millions of pictures of us growing up and while on vacation?"

He thought about my question a minute while cutting into his hot steak sandwich. "Yes, but the really important stuff we have pictures of. Do you remember the picture from Niagara Falls?"

"Sure, I wonder if it's still around."

My dad and me at Niagara Falls, 1969

I was fifteen when we went to Niagara Falls. We went on many family vacations: Washington, DC, Gettysburg, Atlanta, Georgia, and northern Michigan each summer.

My dad didn't like tourist-type things. However, when we were leaving Niagara Falls, he saw this display where you could get your picture in a fake barrel going over the falls.

Dad stopped us all and said, "Hey, Tommy and I have to get a picture taken of us in this barrel." We were all shocked because my dad always said these things were a rip-off, $20 for a fake picture. But this time he insisted—because the barrel featured the word *Daredevil*. He said I was his entrepreneurial daredevil and someday I would be a successful business tycoon.

So up he and I stepped and had this classic picture taken. He reminded me often that, as an entrepreneur, you are sometimes like a daredevil in a barrel going over the Falls. He would say, "Have faith, my boy, and hold on."

However, he would go on and advise me, "Review all the risks and potential rewards. Make your plans, apply them, and move with great determination."

At lunch I reminded him of this funny picture. He said again that he was never big on tourist traps, but when he saw the fake barrel cutout, he knew we had to take the picture. It was perfect, he said, because he knew someday I would be a rocking and rolling entrepreneur. The daredevil picture would prove he knew it was my destiny!

Years later, after I was nominated for "Entrepreneur of the Year," my dad found this old picture and had it framed for me. Wow—the insight only a parent can have about his children.

At this lunch, I suggested we have a professional take a portrait of our whole family. My dad got us all organized and scheduled the photo outing. Shortly after this lunch, he also purchased a top-of-the-line camera, took a photography class, and starting taking pictures of everything.

Gotshall family portrait, 1980
Me, my mom Marian, brother Rob, my dad, and sister Kathy

11

Preparation

One Friday, Dad and I talked at length about why the Gotshall kids were so successful with high school politics. First, my sister, Kathy, was elected as her class vice president; then my brother, Rob, was elected class president.

I felt there were two main reasons for this, and my dad had something to do with both of them. When elections came around each spring for the following school year, each candidate was allowed to hang up campaign posters around the school. My dad's real passion was art and layout graphic art. His first job was as a graphic artist for the *Ann Arbor News*. He was great at it, but eventually went on to advertising because being a graphic artist didn't pay very well.

Still, my dad was a natural artist, and he volunteered to make our campaign posters. They were works of art with catchy slogans on them. Compared with the Gotshall family posters, all the other candidates' posters lining the halls looked like they were made by third graders.

The other reason the Gotshall kids succeed in school elections was the campaign oral presentation and debate. The day before the election, the school would hold an assembly for candidate speeches. Each candidate would be allotted five minutes to detail his or her qualifications. After that, the candidates for the senior class offices would have a lively debate.

Three teachers would ask questions that were submitted by the student body. Questions would range from: "As class president, how would you improve the food in the school cafeteria?" to great ones like: "Should students be allowed to leave during lunch hour to go into town and do whatever they want?"

The other major Gotshall advantage was related to my dad's experience as a sales executive. He made presentations all the time and felt it was a required talent for his kids. Starting the week before any of our debates, Dad staged the school assembly in our living room, complete with a podium and chairs. We were required to make our speech and then listen to his endless critique. Then the fun would start with him firing questions and debating with each of us.

After participating in this banter when my siblings were running for office, I was very prepared, to say the least, when my turn finally rolled around. When it came time for the real debate, there were not any questions I hadn't dealt with. Plus my dad loved to debate all aspects of an issue. Between the great posters and our preparedness, no one had a chance against the Gotshalls. Most kids were nervous to start and would stumble badly during the debate. My dad believed in being over-prepared for these types of events in one's life. I clearly remember him saying, "Assume you will be debating against a member of the U.S. Congress who has been doing this for thirty years. He is well-versed on all topics and has the heart of a lion. Never take your competition for granted." I told my dad they would be too old to run for senior class president. He just ignored my remarks and we would go back to practice. I won the position of senior class president in a landslide.

At lunch, I told my dad that, even though it was a pain at the time, he was correct. This early training in presentation and debate served me well when I became an entrepreneur.

You will give many presentations if you run your own business, even if you don't specialize in sales. You will present your business plans to bankers at some time for funding. It is critical to have the skills necessary to clearly explain the genius of your idea. These presentations will potentially make or break even the launch of your dream.

12

Two Sides

It was April 1985 and the Masters Golf Tournament was being played, which meant spring was in full swing. Both my dad and I loved watching sports. During one Friday lunch that spring, my dad asked me the following: "What do you think of the epic battles of Magic v. Bird, Ali v. Fraser, and Palmer v. Nicholas?"

I replied, "They were interesting and entertaining to watch."

He went on, "The world of an entrepreneur is also an epic battle, progress versus complacency."

As an entrepreneur, you take action and move the bar. You bring movement and progress to society. Most entrepreneurs bring very positive advancements to the world. It's their chosen vocation and their responsibility.

Levi Strauss gave us Levi's.

Bill Gates with Microsoft brought the world home computers.

Bill Pulte of Pulte Homes provided affordable homes to the masses.

Tom Monahan with Domino's Pizza gave us fast home delivery of pizza.

Many entrepreneurs are successful—and sometimes wealthy— because of what they provide. They will rise or fall based on their offering. They are daredevils willing to put themselves out there for the world to see. And society will vote for their product or service based on their acceptance. My dad told me you owe the world your ideas and inspiration. Push forward for the good of mankind. One side is success, fame, and wealth and the other side is failure, period.

13

Off to College

Lunch with my dad was always an adventure. Seldom did either of us have a specific topic we wanted to talk about. We just jumped in and ran in a number of different directions following many tangents.

On this particular day, we talked about when I went off to college. I was the baby of the family and thereby the last to leave home. My dad said, "I was both sad and a little glad to drop you off." My mom, on the other hand, was depressed that her last child was leaving the family roost. I was ready to be a college guy. The parties, new girls, and freedom were beckoning me.

All those years of swimming had paid off as well, as I was also accepted on to the Michigan State University swim team. Yet I was already burned out on swimming and did not last very long on the team. I quit and instead tried out for the MSU Crew Team (rowing) with a number of other swimmers.

Although I had never rowed before, all those years of swimming had developed my upper body and I made the crew team. I rowed on the four-man and eight-man teams. Our four-man team won the Mid-American Regatta and qualified to compete in the 1976 Olympic trials in Boston.

We had a great time rowing with the "big boys" at the trials. Although we finished in the middle of the pack, it was a fabulous experience. I met many great athletes and had a few beers as well.

I always felt participating in sports taught and instilled discipline in players. These same attributes are also incredibly important in an entrepreneur.

After both my freshman and sophomore years, I returned home and got a summer job. I had turned my remaining Gotshall Maintenance customers over to another budding entrepreneur when I went off to college and so now had to work for someone else rather than myself. As I've already discussed, this was not the first time I was an employee for someone else.

These summer jobs were not the best jobs, but they paid. After my freshman year, I worked for the Plymouth DPW (Department of Public Works). They put me in the graveyard. No kidding, the city owned the cemetery and the summer kids got those jobs. Our job was to mow the entire grounds and dig graves on days of funerals. My dad loved that I had landed this job. He knew if I had any doubts about finishing college, this would cement it; he was right.

When my dad would get home from work and before I was heading to the disco (yes, it was the disco era; we were all John Travolta), he would ask, "How's the mowing for the city going, or did somebody die?"

He thought this was very funny, and ironic. I made more money when I was a kid mowing the neighbors' lawns than now, same work less money. The one constant was the smell of freshly cut grass. I loved the smell because it has a clean, moist odor just like after it rains. To this day, whenever I smell freshly cut grass or a grilled steak sandwich, I think of my dad. I was never so happy when that summer came to an end and I could return to Michigan State.

That summer I noted that cutting grass as an employee did not bring the same sense of satisfaction I felt when working and succeeding on my own. This discovery would fuel my entrepreneurial quest my entire life. I always learned a lot when working for others, yet already I knew I would never be completely satisfied in that role.

Michigan State University Four-Man Crew
Mid-American Regatta Champions
I'm pictured front left

14

Money and Friends

"When it comes to loaning money . . . don't. A great friendship can quickly become a hated business partner you don't want."

—Robert H. Gotshall Sr.

During our lunches, my dad would usually toss out an open probe to get us rolling on a topic. This day the talk was about loaning money to friends. I quickly said, "No way, I will never make that mistake again."

I reminded my dad about both his lesson and my bad experience.

During the summer of 1975, I returned home from college and was working at Sun Plastics, a small, local manufacturing plant. I was the college kid and I had made a few suggestions to the owner about how we could become more productive with our spring coating process, so he put me in charge as the night foreman with three employees. Our job was to coat large front-wheel springs for trucks. We hung the springs with vice-grips on a hanging conveyer belt, heated them to two hundred degrees, pulled them off, and then put them in a vat of plastic powder. The powder would stick to the red hot spring; then we would hang them on another belt for drying. Nasty work, and probably not great for my lungs either. The smell that filled the factory air was like old burnt tires.

One of "my" workers was going to move away from the area. He had an Opel Kadett that was ten years old, not in great shape, and he wanted to get rid of it. I wasn't really interested. The next month, I was finishing up at Sun Plastics with plans to take a week off to vacation in Colorado before heading back to MSU where I didn't need a car. His last night on the job he said, "Just make me an offer." I looked over the car and after a quick drive around the block, I offered him $100. All I had on me was $108. He said, "Sold." I thought, *Oh great, what am I going to do with this car?* For the next few weeks my buddies and I bummed around in it having a grand time. I mentioned to one of them that I was leaving for Colorado in a few days and I wanted to sell the car.

When I bought the car for $100, I figured I could drive it for a month and then sell it for a profit. One of my friends, Mike, said, "I love this car. Would you take $150 for it?" I just knew when I bought it that it was a great investment. I said sure. He went on, "I don't have all the cash. In fact, I won't have any until after you head to Colorado. How about if I drop it off at your parents' house—$50 on Monday after you leave, then $100 on Friday? So by the time you come back, you will have the $150 waiting for you." I hesitated, but went for the deal.

At the time my dad thought it was a bad idea: "What if he wrecks the car or decides he can't pay you for it?"

Great point, but I reminded him of another piece of advice he had given me: "When you agree to a deal with someone and shake his hand, you had better live up to your end of the bargain." I told him, "We shook hands and I'm giving him the keys tomorrow."

Dad said, "Well at least keep the title until you get the full $150."

So I dropped off the car and keys. Mike was thrilled and said, "No worries, I will make payments so when you get back, the deal will be completed." Off I went feeling like both of us got a good deal.

I called home on Wednesday to check in with my parents. No payment had been made. Rats! When I returned the following week,

I was sure the $150 would be waiting for me. No such luck. I was in disbelief. How could a good friend not fulfill his end of the bargain? I called his parents' house, where he lived, and no one answered. This was also before answering machines and cell phones. The phone in those days just rang and rang. After a few calls, I got his dad on the line. He said he would pass the message on to Mike. No call back after two days. Now I was mad as hell. I got the other set of keys I still had and rode my bike over to his house. The car was there, so I knocked on the door; no answer. Now I'm crazy mad— my good friend was screwing me. I put my bike in the backseat, got in the car, and laid on the horn; still no Mike. So off I drove with my car. That night when my dad got home from work, he saw my great investment sitting in the driveway.

In he came and proclaimed, "It looks like you are the proud owner of a great German automobile the Opel Kadett!" My dad never buried me or told me I was dumb to trust a great ex-friend. He did say, "You were smart to keep the title of the car, because you had the right to go get it. When it comes to money, always protect yourself with a written contract, never a verbal agreement. When it comes to loaning money (this was sort of a loan) to someone . . . don't do it. Period." He said I learned a very valuable lesson for only $100.

Just think if it had been $1,000 or $10,000 or even more; just say no. The next day, I took my investment up to a used car lot in Plymouth, Tyme Auto. He offered me $65 for the car. I agreed, signed over the title, took the cash, and rode my bike home.

Finally, after two more days, my pal called. "Where's my car?" he asked. "I have $75, and I can pay you the rest in a week." I asked him about the original deal we had, and he said he got a little jammed up. I told him I was going back to MSU the next day and ran out of time. "And speaking of time," I said, "the car's up at Tyme Auto; go buy it if you want it.

The next time I saw my pal, I did feel differently toward him. I did not hate him, but I felt he screwed me around and was a jerk. He also told me he went up to Tyme Auto the day he called me and the car had already been sold for $350. Bad deal for everyone, except Mr. Tyme Auto.

15

Gotshall Painting

"The future never just happened. It was created."
—Will Durant, (1885-1981),
American writer and philosopher

On one particular Friday, I was beat up from a tough week of selling computers. As I dragged myself into lunch with Dad, he could clearly see I was worn out. He started out, "I know selling can wear you out, but remember the painting business you started while at Michigan State?"

After living in the dorm for two years, a group of us got together to find a house off campus and rented it for our junior year. A lot of students did this. So we moved into the rental. The rent was high, but it was within walking distance to campus.

It was a twelve-month lease, so I planned on staying for the summer. I asked the landlord if he needed any work done during the summer. I had two classes and so I couldn't take on a full-time eight-to-five weekday job. He asked me if I could paint. I replied, "Like an artist?" Both my brother and dad did oil painting, so that's what automatically popped into my head. No, he meant like house painting. I paused and thought about my uncle Ray who was a house painter, but I had never done painting myself. I asked him, "For your rentals properties?" He replied, "Yeah." How hard could this be, I thought. I answered him, "Yeah, I've been painting for years!" Just like that, he turned and looked up at the house we were living in, a white two-story house with green shutters. "Let's start with this one," he said. I thought, *Uh-oh, big house.*

He went on, "I will pay for the paint. I have an account at Capital Paint. You scrape, prep, and paint one coat and complete it in one week. I will pay you $450 for labor." Then he turned, got in his car, and was off. Now I had done many jobs: snow shoveling, raking, mowing, baling hay, stocking suits, selling suits, but nothing like house painting. I called home to get my uncle Ray's phone number for consulting.

"Good luck with this one and be careful," my dad advised me. My uncle was great. He was a professional house painter in Grosse Pointe with wealthy clients who expected the best. He told me working on a ladder is like being a ballerina. No kidding, balance, up on your toes, up and down all day. I replied, "I row on the MSU crew team. I'm sure I can handle this."

So he explained what I'd need:

- Equipment: Rent a ladder for the first job, since it may be your only job.
- Scraper: Get the best one.
- Buckets: Get two or three.
- Paintbrushes: Get a good one.

He went on with his advice, "This is a college rental property. Just scrape off the big chunks of peeling paint; don't bother with sand paper." Uncle Ray told me this job should take two to three days preparation one day, two days of painting, tops. I pounded out the job in four and a half days. Not great quality but new paint was now on the house. As for my balance debate, my uncle was correct. My legs were killing me. My calves were sore in muscles I didn't know existed.

Mr. Williams, the landlord, came by to "inspect" my completed project and to pay up.

He pulled up in his Cadillac and rolled down the window: "Gotshall, come here." He handed me a check for $450 and asked if I could do another house. Most every muscle in my body said no way. I asked if there would be more. He laughed and said he could keep me busy for two summers with the number of houses he had that needed work.

Just like that, my rental house painting business was off the ground. The income was based on how many houses I could paint. The quality was, well, not so important. I purchased a ladder and a turquoise 1965 Ford pickup truck, a three-on-the-tree manual, for $350; it wasn't much to look at, but it ran like a top.

Getting the ladder, paint, and equipment around was a real pain before I had the truck. After a few more houses, I called Mr. Williams for a meeting.

He said he would meet me for fifteen minutes over a cup of coffee at Beggers Banquet, just off campus. I called my dad for advice. He said, "This property owner is probably most interested is getting his rentals painted fast. I'm sure how they look is also important; however, not like his own house." My dad's advice was to try and make a deal to get all his houses. He also said, "Try and learn something about the rental business."

I went prepared, with a pad of paper and a pen. I asked Mr. Williams how many rentals he needed painted that summer. He said thirty, give or take. I told him I would do every one. He said there was no way that I could pull that off.

This was my plan: Hire two scrapers and buy two more ladders. The first house we will all scrape, so I can show my employees (two of my roommates also without jobs) just how it's done. Then I will send them on to the next house to scrape and I will stay back and do the painting. About when I would be done painting, they would be done scraping on house two. I would start painting and they would move to house three to scrape. I got painting down to one and a half days. So every three to three and a half days, we could complete one house. Six days a week equals two houses. We had twelve weeks left that summer.

I figured twenty-four houses, no problem. And when school started, we could find time during the week and weekend to finish the remaining six houses. After all, we could all use the money.

He said, "What about rain?" In Michigan, we can have a lot of rain in the summer.

I replied, "No problem. As long as we have all thirty house addresses, we will scrape on rain days and paint on sunny days." I thought, *I will have three ladders, and men on ladders equals income.*

The meeting lasted over an hour and Mr. Williams, being an entrepreneur himself, liked and respected my plan. He hired me that day and provided all the addresses. We agreed that I would get paid after every two houses were painted, or every Friday.

My dad suggested I prepare a contract covering all the details.

1. Home addresses
2. Payment amount with dates
3. Who paid for expenses: he covered paint and I covered other materials
4. Contract time frame

He also said both of us should sign the contract. I wasn't so sure about this. I did not want to push my luck. However, my dad said this would protect both of us and make things clear. Also as a businessman, Mr. Williams dealt with contracts all the time.

So I wrote my very first contract, a one-pager with lines for both of us to sign at the bottom. I think Mr. Williams was impressed that "I" thought of this, and he was happy to sign it.

I kept a ledger that summer and the numbers worked out like this:

Income
$450 per house
32 houses
$14,400 gross

Expenses
Bruce: $3,000
Steve: $2,500
Equipment: two ladders, $400
Misc.: $300
Total: $6,200

Net profit: $8,200

It was hard work with many ten-hour days. I learned a lot that summer, including that I didn't want to paint houses for a living or even do any manual labor. The experience convinced me to get a college degree and encouraged me to be the boss. Even though I knew that I didn't want to stay in the house-painting business, I made more money that summer than any other college student I knew. Working for myself and being an entrepreneur instilled the lifelong quest in me.

The other very important take-away from that summer was knowledge about the student rental business. My dad sat down with me and developed a list of questions for Mr. Williams about the business. As I built a working relationship with him, one pay day I proposed, "I would like to buy you dinner after work one day and ask a few questions about the rental business." He replied, "Sure. How's next Friday [pay day]?"

After work, I was always a mess—paint, sweat, and grime. My dad suggested I put on a shirt and tie for the occasion. He said this will elevate me in Mr. Williams's mind from college painting grunt to a budding businessman. As usual, my dad was right.

Mr. Williams did a double take on me when we met for dinner. He was used to seeing me unshaven, dirty, and with paint covering my clothes, hands, and face. "What's with the tie?" he asked. I told him I felt this was a business meeting and I should dress appropriately.

After a beer (the drinking age was eighteen back then), I pulled out my pad of paper and started in on my questions.

Step 1: Break the ice.

Step 2: Ask general questions.

Step 3: Ask specific questions (the most important).

I started, "How do you like owning rentals and why did you get started?" Important note: My dad said ask (open probe) and then shut up and listen; never, ever interrupt.

Mr. Williams told me he used to be a teacher, making $18,750 a year with the summer off. A fellow teacher owned one student rental near MSU and he made $3,000 a year on that rental. He learned that student ghettos would provide passive income—income from an investment that doesn't require daily effort, like stocks and bonds. He explained, "The trick is to buy houses close to campus. Most students don't have cars and they don't want to be over fifteen minutes by bike to class."

He told me in great detail how he purchased his first house for no money down, which was a $55,000 house. The math for the income looked like this:

- Rent: $2,500/month
- Mortgage: $1,500
- Taxes: $300
- Maintenance: $150
- Net $550/month x 12=$6,600/year

I realized why he was no longer a teacher. With thirty-two rentals generating an average yearly income of $5,000, this represented annual income of $160,000 versus his former teaching salary of $18,750.

He told me it wasn't always so pure. You put six to eight college kids in a house, and they beat the crap out of the place. He would get one and a half months' rent (as the law allows) for a security deposit, but hot water tanks and kitchen appliances just wear out fast.

I didn't ask him just how much he made, but he offered the following:

"After I owned five houses, I was making more on rental properties than teaching. I made the break, quit, and proceeded to buy, buy, buy."

After this meeting, I tried to convince my dad to buy a rental house. He came up to see me at my house. We had a rule among us six roommates: no parents in the house. We called ourselves the "Beal Street Bombers" and, yes, we were typical college students in 1977.

Well, I warned everyone my dad was coming in. My dad proceeded to look around. There was a certain feel to the house—four empty beer kegs in the backyard that was mostly dirt, three to four broken windows in the back, and the kitchen was pretty dirty as were the bathrooms.

At lunch that day, my dad said, "Interesting business model but no way! You will graduate and I will be stuck dealing with it." We debated; I wanted to do it but he was the one with the money and credit, not me.

He said, "Why don't you come back to this area someday after graduation? If you still feel it's a good opportunity, jump in. Remember, persistence is a key building block. Also sometimes opportunity takes time."

16

Grandpa Gotshall

On one Friday, I noticed my dad was wearing a tie that must have been ten years old. My dad was handsome and always dressed well. I asked him, "Dad, just how old is that tie you are wearing?"

His reply was, "Well it's a few years old but still in style and looking perfect. Why wouldn't I continue to wear it?" My dad was German and frugal. He learned from a pro: my grandmother, his mother. My grandfather didn't earn a lot of money. However, they had a lot of money.

Grandpa Gotshall was born in 1892 in Pennsylvania. In the 1920s nobody in the Unites States liked the Germans. The only jobs they could get were working in the coal mines. Horrible working conditions and lousy pay. In a coal mine accident, my grandfather lost his leg—a coal car ran over it.

Growing up, I never knew this. He walked with a prosthesis most of his life. I only found this out near the end of his life. He was eighty-two and in the hospital dying from "black lung" and many strokes when I went to visit him. He was sleeping in his bed, and I noticed the outline of the cover over his left leg ended at his knee.

I asked a nurse who came by, "Where's my grandpa's leg?"

She replied, "In the closet!"

I was twenty, not a kid, and I'm sure she thought I would have known about his leg. She probably figured I wanted to know where his prosthesis was. After she left, I walked over, opened the closet, and sure enough, leaning in the corner, was his fake leg. It was made out of wood and had leather straps that were used to attach it to his upper leg. His shoe was on it! I couldn't believe it.

I remembered my dad advising me not to tell the other kids about my asthma. I realized this outlook must have come from my very proud grandfather. I remember he even played kickball with us as kids in the backyard. What a shock to see his leg in that closet.

Three days after visiting my grandfather, without discussion with my parents, my buddy Schwartz and I decided to go to Colorado to see my brother. You know, young and in need of adventure. We just needed to bust out. About halfway there, somewhere in Iowa, we called home from a pay phone to "advise" our parents of our plans. Instead, my parents advised me that my grandfather had passed away that morning. Schwartz's dad told him he was going to "beat" his ass when he got home. He said he hope we enjoyed Colorado, because he was going to die when he returned.

My dad said, "Your grandfather loved you very much and understood the pain you went through with asthma." This made sense to me now, after seeing his leg in the closet. About our trip, he said, "If going to Colorado was important to you, he would understand."

Are you kidding? No screaming or demanding. It was my decision, what pressure.

At one of our lunches, I asked my dad about this exchange. He said, "As an adult, you have to make many decisions in life. Hard ones." He figured it was time I grew up and learned how to make them and deal with the consequences. He said he also figured I would make the correct decision.

I got off the phone to find that Schwartz was already flirting with a couple of local girls, farmers' daughters. I turned to him and said, "We have to go back tonight."

Thinking I was kidding, he said, "Shut up!"

There we stood with our two new friends, me convincing him to do something neither of us really wanted to do—return home. But we did. The girls offered to give us a full tank of gas. We had begun this adventure underfunded. We all hopped in the car and drove into the country. It turned out one of the girls really was a farmer's daughter, and farms had their own gas tanks for tractors and other farm equipment. We pulled around behind the barn; they jumped out, opened the combination lock, pulled down the pump handle, and filled us up.

Schwartz just couldn't believe we were saying good-bye ten minutes later. It was a long drive home, fourteen hours. We agreed we would head back to Colorado in a few days.

Schwartz dropped me off at eight o'clock the next morning. When I walked in, my mom burst into tears and my dad shook my hand. I knew Schwartz was getting a different reception. I showered, shaved, got on a suit, and went to my grandfather's funeral.

After the funeral, my grandmother, a firecracker of a woman, bright blue-eyes and flame-red hair, approached me about my escapade and trip halfway to Colorado. She said, "You are a wild one with great potential, just like your grandfather. Come over next week and I will tell you his life story and how to become rich." She asked about my trip and so I told her about the two girls we met and about our little adventure with them. She laughed out loud (she loved to laugh). Everybody was pleased to see my grandmother had found something to laugh about that day. Nobody knew why, but they all felt better because she was laughing.

My dad with his father, Walter Gotshall, pictured in 1942

17

Grandma's Wisdom

The week after my grandfather's funeral, I accepted my grandmother's invitation and dropped in for lunch. She answered the door wearing a dress with an apron over it, which was her uniform. My grandmother was always cooking, something she loved and was great at. The smell of sauerkraut hit me in the nose. She made everything from scratch; no frozen, boxed, or canned food came out of her kitchen. During Thanksgiving at her house, we all joked that she went out and shot the turkey herself.

That afternoon, we had sauerkraut, sausage, fresh pears, potato pancakes, and apple pie. After lunch, she poured me a glass of whole milk and handed me a bowl of ice cream topped with peppermint. I was already about to explode. My grandfather was six feet tall, no belly, and in great shape to the day he died. How did he do that, I joked to my grandmother; why didn't gramps weigh 300 pounds? My grandfather looked just like the General from the old movie *White Christmas* with Bing Crosby and Danny Kaye. Not only that, he acted like him as well—proud and very loving in a quiet way. Grandma said he never smoked, even though smoking was glorified back in that era. He had a small glass of port wine on Saturday night (only one) and they walked after dinner every night. Maybe that's the trick because my grandfather loved to eat.

My grandma asked me if I wanted to be rich. I replied, "Of course; doesn't everyone?" She asked if I wanted to know how to become wealthy.

So now, with great anticipation, I'm waiting for the true great secret to great wealth.

I said, "Yes!"

She told me, "Hard work and save 20 percent of your gross pay. That's it." And, "Oh, by the way, have a plan at the start of each year. Write down five goals for the year and how much you want to save and invest." Same thing my dad told me. However, she did add a twist to this advice. She said, "In addition to working a full-time job, you must own something that generates income."

"Like a business?" I asked. "Well if that is true, what about you and Gramps?"

She explained, "Well we did follow that strategy." It turns out my grandparents had two strategies. Before this day, I knew nothing of either one. My grandmother went on to tell me that she and my grandfather had owned a dance hall with another couple, Edna and Norm. I'm sure my mouth dropped open upon hearing this news. My grandmother explained how it worked: She and Edna cooked all the food. My grandpa and Norm set up and cleaned. They also made money on the bar. They purchased beer and wine and had a cash bar at all occasions. They rented the place out on Thursday, Friday, Saturday, and Sundays nights for weddings, retirement parties, promotional parties, etc. My grandfather also had a full-time job running the heating and electrical infrastructure at one of the large high schools in Detroit. Their second source of income all went into savings.

My grandmother went on to tell me that she read the *Wall Street Journal* every day and invested their savings in stocks and bonds, mostly blue-chip equities (stocks). She said she liked utilities and S.S. Kresge. S.S. Kresge later became Kmart, and they made a fortune. That's why they could live in a big house in Grosse Pointe with all the auto executives, plus have a house in Boca Raton, Florida. Hard work, save, have a second source of income, and invest wisely. My grandma said, "The more, Doe-Ray-Me the better." That's what she called money.

When I left Grandma's house that day, I had a completely different view of my grandparents.

Often, people idolize the wrong people in our country: Actors and musicians who use drugs and behave poorly. The best role models should be individuals who set a good example and accomplish good things. Also, our elders can be a great source of ideas and inspiration.

If you have a grandfather and/or grandmother living, go have lunch with them tomorrow, not next week.

We can learn many things from our parents and grandparents.

Ask many questions and listen to their advice on life. Once they have passed away, so too will all their experience and insight.

My Grandmother Gotshall in 1974

18

Singing in the Rain

One Friday shortly after the Academy Awards, Dad and I spent our lunch discussing the movies that won the Oscars. It was 1991, and *Silence of the Lambs* won movie of the year and Anthony Hopkins and Jodie Foster won best actor and actress for the same movie. My dad said he didn't enjoy most of the movies being produced these days. I asked, "What type of movies do you like?"

To this he replied, "You know. *It's a Wonderful Life* with Jimmy Stewart; *The Wizard of Oz* with Judy Garland; *White Christmas* with Bing Crosby and Danny Kay. But my favorite movie hands down is *Singing in the Rain* with Gene Kelly."

When I asked him why, he told me he liked feel-good movies.

He even said he had a favorite scene: "It's raining hard and Gene Kelly is singing and dancing with an umbrella that he mostly doesn't use. The song he is singing is Singing in the Rain."

My dad hated so many of the typical movies made these days— scary, bloody, sad. He couldn't understand why he or most people would pay good money to watch bad things happen. He clearly understood the real world, but he preferred feel-good movies. Singing and dancing with people in love and living happily ever after. The other twist is that my dad was the most positive person in the world. He always looked at the positive in every person and situation. And why not? Yes, there are bad people, and bad things will happen to good people. But my dad's perspective was, be and stay positive and happy. A strong positive mental attitude will help you through many tough situations. Once you go negative, it's hard to get the positive spirit going again. Plus, remaining positive feels better. Like Gene Kelly singing and dancing with the rain pouring down on him. It is going to rain and you can't control or stop it. How you deal with it is up to you. Stay the course and be positive at all times. It will catch on with everyone around you. This PMA—positive mental attitude—was just how my dad lived his life.

In my entire life, I never remember my dad being bitter or even mad about anything. Being positive at all times is also very important for entrepreneurs. Deal with adversity or negative situations and move on.

Keep singing . . . even in the rain.

Part II

Bootstrapping New Ventures

"When one door closes, another opens; but we often look so long and so regretfully upon the closed door that we do not see the one which has opened for us."

—Alexander Graham Bell (1847-1922),
inventor and scientist

19

Perspective

My dad got philosophical during one Friday lunch and said, "The way you think and react to everything today is based on your life experiences." He recognized that genetics played a small part in your life. He felt that your upbringing and education, along with your peers and all your life experiences, played a much bigger part. He also felt that negative or even "bad" things had a proportionately greater effect on us than the positive things we experienced.

I felt this was very true in dealing with other people. After getting "burned" by a few people, one is inclined not to trust others. But I remembered what my dad told me, "As an entrepreneur or just a member of the human race, you must learn to trust most people. Don't be cynical and non-trusting of everyone. However, question and evaluate important people in your life."

Learn from all your situations in life. All my experiences have helped shape and form my opinions and outlook. My entrepreneurial experiences started the first day I dealt with my neighbor Mr. Simmons. When I agreed to shovel his snow for "two bits" and he ended up giving me an additional three dollars, I learned a lesson.

I learned to understand my pricing and to expect a fair price for my services. I also learned that people can take advantage of you if you are inexperienced. Fortunately for me, Mr. Simmons was interested in helping me grow and was more than fair. Many times, my dad pointed out the need to deal with any adversity and make it a positive outcome. Mr. Simmons, and most people, are good as well as fair. Just know these are the types of people you want to surround yourself with, work with, and be friends with.

Dad also told me, "Think about what my father dealt with, the loss of his leg at the age of twenty. The opportunity to work in the coal mines of Pennsylvania was lost with his leg. So what he did was move to Michigan and start over, where nobody knew about his leg." Although my dad was plagued with problems with his arm, he never let it stop him from doing what he wanted. He took up golf and just made it work. I remember when I was dealing with asthma, he said, "You can tell everyone or no one. It is up to you and you alone." But he also told me, "Tell your friends and they will look at you differently. That's okay, but once you tell one person, everyone will know about your 'asthmatic condition.'" I chose not to tell anyone, so all the people reading this book who have known me for years are now finding out what I struggled with all those years.

The two reasons I never told anyone was, first, I didn't want to be looked at differently. Both kids and adults want to fit in. Whether it's in a group in the neighborhood or school or on a team, I just wanted to be part of it and included. The other reason was I did not want anyone to feel sorry for me and single me out. The neighborhood kids called me wheeze, but none of them knew just why I wheezed. My brother didn't tell anyone because he wanted to protect me; plus, he didn't want to have that poor sick kid brother. When I missed an entire school year because I was homeschooled, the rumors were that I was sent off to military school or I was sent to a school for smart kids. The following year when I returned to school, no one asked about it. The only comment was that I was lucky to have missed the stupid third grade at Smith Elementary School.

Perspective is what makes each of us unique. I chose to take my unique and individual prospective and become an entrepreneur. I become charged up and very determined when I create a business. From snow shoveling and lawn maintenance, to house painting and then rental property ownership, I loved the creation and building process. I dealt with adversity and success the exact same way: head-on. Part of the feeling and determination to do this may have come from the need to prove I could do it. Was this ego? Maybe. All very successful people have a "big ego."

Every person will experience some failure in life as well as great disappointment. I found a way to learn from my mistakes and prospered.

A critical building block for all entrepreneurs is the ability to compartmentalize and keep everything in proper perspective, both good things as well as trying situations.

Occasionally I would have a day in which everything would go wrong. I would call my dad and proclaim: "This is just too hard and a pain. I don't think I'm cut out for being an entrepreneur." Or sometimes the opposite would happen and we would secure all the deals we were working on and every employee was performing over the top. On these calls I would proclaim: "I'm a genius and the greatest entrepreneur known to mankind! I'm going to hire twenty more people and expand our operations into the entire Midwest." His advice in both situations was always the same. He would say, "Both good things and bad thing will come your way. Hold on, take tonight to think things over, and develop a plan for dealing with your situation. Balance all the pros and cons; then make what you feel is the best decision and move on with it. However, never make any decision hastily and without looking at all sides of your decision." As always, his advice was spot on and it forced me to think clearly before deciding anything.

20

The Real World

One Friday, my dad asked me what I learned from my job experiences after graduating from college.

I graduated from Michigan State University with a degree in Fisheries and Wildlife—really. My specialization was Ichthyology. I had classes such as Fisheries Management, Restoration Ecology, and Limnology (the study of water)—not to mention two years of Organic Chemistry, Physics, Calculus, and Biology!

It was a very difficult curriculum, but I wanted to save the world's ecosystem. The only problem was there were no jobs available in that field. I feel most universities do a poor job of advising its student population of the "Real World."

Colleges and universities are large businesses. My degree cost more than $80,000, in today's dollars. Private schools cost $180,000 to $250,000. These institutions have many different degrees to offer and they must put "butts in seats." Many degrees offer little or no post-graduation opportunity. Most schools do degree consulting but little job and income consulting. However, shame on me for not investigating my prospects long before declaring my major. Even today, when I go on the MSU website and research my degree, it sounds like a lot of exciting opportunities exist. Yet what I found after graduating was the following:

The State of Michigan hires one person a year in the Department of Natural Resources. MSU alone graduates more than fifty-five kids a year with this degree. I did find a job with the Environmental Protection Agency (EPA) making about twenty dollars an hour. However, the job was available only because of a grant, and when the grant ended six months later, I was out of a job. The alternative to another job search was to go back to school and get my master's—great but still very few jobs. Or I could get my PhD and then teach. Make no mistake; I believe a college degree is a minimum requirement today. However, it is wise to do your own research and career planning. Develop a clear understanding of your post-undergraduate and advanced degree opportunities. I feel the best degrees for an entrepreneur are in the business school in areas like accounting, finance, or business management.

Despite the lack of opportunity in my chosen field, I had a great time attending MSU. Everything about my time there was terrific. The education, social interaction, and athletic experiences were all better than I ever expected. A big part of who I am today is because of my time at MSU. Attending college is a critical part of developing as a person. Outside of the classroom you learn many life lessons while having a lot of fun.

To answer my dad's question, I started by saying, "You were correct that getting a degree in 'Frogs, Ducks, and Fish' was a bad decision. I should have listened to you and looked at finance or management or any number of things." As always, my dad put a positive spin on it: "Maybe, but the most important thing was you completed your degree and now have a great job in the fastest growing industry, computers."

After the short-lived EPA job, I decided to get my master's degree in hospital administration. I was accepted into the program at the University of Michigan, the same institution that probably saved my life years earlier with their groundbreaking asthma treatment. Once I learned I was accepted, the fall semester was nine months away. A university counselor suggested I work in a hospital to get some practical experience while I was waiting. I got a job at Port Huron General Hospital in Port Huron, Michigan. It was fascinating; they had me work in every department from maternity to surgery. I was a prep orderly for all types of surgery. I also worked on the pediatrics' floor, which brought back many memories of my time in the hospital as a young child. In the end, after all this, I decided not to pursue a master's degree in hospital administration because I couldn't see myself in that career.

My dad got me an interview with Mr. Ray Post, the regional director for Chevrolet, a division of General Motors. We had a great interview. He told me if I wanted to work as a district manager with Chevy, I would first have to get a sales job at a Chevrolet dealership. He felt the experience would greatly help me. The DM position involved calling on the dealerships and acting as a liaison between them and the corporation. This made sense to me, and besides, I felt it was a required step to get my foot in the door at one of the largest and best corporations in the world, General Motors.

I worked for Lou LaRiche Chevrolet in Plymouth for nine months. Each month, I would mail Mr. Post my sales results and general impressions of the business, all positive. I had a great experience and enjoyed the dealership. They tried to convince me to stay on when I received an offer to move up, but I was ready for Corporate America.

My new job was calling on the presidents of Chevrolet dealerships and advising them on what was on the way from the corporation. Plus, I was supposed to convince them to order more car and truck inventory. I would get my quota each week by product line, and by Friday, I had to move all the product inventory. I was to convince these very successful entrepreneurs to order more, no matter what.

This experience of calling on and dealing with this group of successful entrepreneurs was a continuation of my E-Education (entrepreneurial). As always, I asked endless questions when it was appropriate to do so. All of these great entrepreneurs were intrigued by my probing. I told them that one day I, too, hoped to become an entrepreneur.

I wanted to find out what made them tick. How did they make decisions and problem solve? What did they think made a great leader? How did they deal with adversity? Who was their coach? How did they set goals; did they consult others, or were they on their own? Why the car business? Many of my series of questions led to other questions. Many of my dealers were over fifty years old and they enjoyed guiding me through this educational process.

They all had a unique style and their own perspective. However, I remember telling my dad they all had some similar points of view and beliefs: "They all had a strong passion for the business. They had opinions about what was good and what was amiss with the industry. They were all car and truck guys. Customer service was the most important part of this business to all of them. They understood how important it was to retain customers. Winning a new customer was probably the toughest part of the business. Their employees were the ones to make or break their business, so they treated them all as well as they could. They wanted to exceed all of their customers' expectations. They had all learned a lot from the foreign auto brand and dealerships. They didn't look at their business as a 9 to 5 occupation. Instead it was 24/7. They seldom talked about their income as their primary motivation. They were all very aware of community activities and had a strong desire to give back."

The more I got to know these individuals, the more I respected them. They were hard-working, passionate, and driven entrepreneurs. I learned a massive amount from them and owe much of my entrepreneurial perspective to them.

At lunch, my dad suggested I keep notes on the things I learned from my experiences. He said, "Someday, you will be in their shoes and you will be further ahead armed with their knowledge and impressions."

21

Whatever It Takes

One Friday in early spring, my dad and I met for lunch. The stock market was starting to make big advancements. Everybody in the market was happy and prosperity was prevalent. Because my grandparents had shown him the positive but conservative approach to using the stock market as a financial instrument of gain, my dad was also very pleased at the direction the market was taking.

As I sat down at the table, my dad beamed: "How about the uptick in the market today?"

I replied, "You have to have money to make money."

He went on, "Aren't you glad you left Chevrolet and pushed to get a better-paying position in computer sales?"

I said, "Yes, it's funny how life can become redirected."

After working at Chevrolet for three years, I became restless. I knew there was more to my career and future than what Chevy could offer.

I decided to pursue work in the computer industry. I was dating a nurse, Marti Sassack. I was forever attracted to nurses, probably something to do with all my contact with them when I was sick as a kid. She was living with two other nurses. Patty, one of her roommates, was dating Craig Bickley, a sales executive in the computer industry. I drove a new Chevy (company car), which I didn't own, lived in an average apartment, and made $19,500 a year.

Craig drove a Cadillac, had an expense account, and wore nice suits while making $70,000 a year.

I wanted a job at that company; plus the automobile industry was tired and static and didn't offer much opportunity for advancement. The regional manager for GM was fifty years old and, after working at the company for twenty-five years, was making what Craig was making.

I understood sales but very little about the computer industry. I convinced Craig to get me an interview just the same. His boss, Lee Hagen, was a go-go guy. After a lot of pushing, he agreed to meet with me. We had a great conversation, but he finished by telling me, "Although I'm very impressed with you, you don't have the experience to get a job as a sales executive in the computer business."

Not again, I thought. This was what had happened at Chevrolet. Now it appeared the computer industry was the same.

Getting your first real job is very tough. Experience is key. When a company hires someone, it is both time consuming and expensive. They must minimize the risk. Hiring someone with experience along with a track record helps reduce the risk. I told Lee I was not going to just walk away and forget about the computer business.

After the interview, I studied and read as much as I could about the industry—trends, new technologies, and developments. Plus, I read and studied everything about MAI, the firm I wanted to work for. It was a public company, so a lot of information was available. I also stayed in touch with Craig.

After about three months, he called and told me a position was opening up. I immediately called Lee and asked for another meeting. I also told him, "Now I have experience plus knowledge." Lee was busy, but I was persistent enough that he agreed to meet. At the meeting, I told him about the industry trends—what was new and hot, and what was dying. I also talked about MAI's balance sheet, new operations, and who they acquired in the past six months. I even quoted the CEO from his opening statement in the annual report.

Lee said, "Wow, very impressive. However, I still need an industry-proven sales executive with a track record selling computer systems."

Now I was energized. I told him very coolly, "Okay, but I will get a job in this industry, maybe working for IBM or HP or some other competitor, and every time we compete, I will do everything I can to win the deal over you and MAI." I stood up and headed for the door.

Lee said, "Now that's the type of 'fire in the belly' we need."

I knew my taking a stand in this way was a big risk. With the wrong type of person, you could destroy any chance you have of being hired on. Yet, in this case, I figured I had nothing to lose. Lee told me he couldn't hire me as a sales executive, but he would bring me in as a sales associate, working for and supporting the sales executives. If I panned out, I could get a sales executive position within six months. I had one final interview with Lee's boss, Herb Galloway. He was stocky, with a brush haircut. Ex-military, hard-nosed guy. I went in a few days later for the interview, and Lee led me in and introduced us. Herb opened, "Is this the bastard who said he would kick our butts working for some other maggot computer company?"

I thought, *Uh, oh.*

Lee replied, "Yes sir, one in the same."

Herb stood up, reached out his hand, and said, "Great, boy, now you are one of us. When you finally get that sales position, I want you to kick every competitor's ass, just like you were going to kick ours. You start Monday and be early." And the interview was over.

I felt the urge to salute, but didn't.

When I got to my car, it took me ten minutes to catch my breath. Finally a break, not a great one, but I had to start somewhere.

Four years of college

Three years at Chevrolet

And now a secretary

My dad had the best perspective, "Decide what industry you want to get in to and go after it—hard." If you have to start sweeping the floors, at least you are in the right position for a potential opportunity. He told me, "Make sure you are the best sales associate they have ever had. Blow them away. Always do extra work and make sure the boss knows it. Check your ego at the door and keep your eye on the prize." The prize for me was to be a sales executive.

After three months, I was promoted to that position. After two and a half years, I became the district sales manager, which was Lee's former position. Years later, I still stay in touch with Herb. He retired long ago and moved back to North Carolina. When I see him, I still have the feeling I should salute. He had a very distinguished career in the service and went to Vietnam, when many young men disagreed with the war and ran off to Canada. Herb didn't question it; he felt it was his obligation to fight for and support the country.

My career in the computer industry started in 1983, at a time when there was an endless amount of innovation going on:

- Microsoft, with the guidance of Bill Gates and Paul Allen, was just beginning to explode.
- Scott McNealy formed Sun Microsystems in 1982 and pioneered open systems and later introduced Java.
- H/P and IBM, plus most major computer manufacturers, were all designing and releasing mini-computers, which revolutionized the entire industry.

As a result, the opportunity for everyone working in the industry was expanding and endless. The wave that took place was unparalleled in the history of the computer industry.

On the day I resigned from Chevrolet, I started down my new direction. I stayed in touch with three other guys I had worked with at Chevy, and after three years one had been laid off, another was in the same position, and one had moved up. However, to reach the regional position with Chevrolet would have taken twenty years and endless moves.

It is very important to evaluate where you are at any given time in your career. It is also important to take a good look at the industry you're in. If you love what you do, or even like what you do, and believe in yourself and the industry, stay put and plan your eventual entrepreneurial escape. On the other hand, if you are in a bad job and bad industry, get out and move on. But don't just quit. Remember how long it took me to get hired at both Chevrolet and MAI? Plus, it is easier to get a new job when you are currently employed. Fair or unfair, this is just a fact.

After working at MAI for five and a half years, I decided the time was right to change gears. MAI sold business and accounting computer systems. The CAD/CAM business was hot due to all the design and engineering the auto industry did in Michigan.

Another colleague from MAI had left to go to Prime Computer two years earlier. They were a public company in the CAD/CAM Industry. I contacted Big Al (Al Violassi) to inquire about any openings in sales. He put me in touch with his boss, Sam Lawrence.

Now that I had experience in sales and management in the computer field, career movement was relatively easy. I contacted Sam and within two weeks and a few interviews I was hired. So now, once again, I was able to save some money because my income began to exceed my expenses.

One Friday, my dad and I were talking money management when he told me the following: "Pay yourself first" with your income. He then explained, "Most people, whether they make 20K, 30K, 40K, 50K, or 75K, are looking to spend it, which makes a lot of sense. Let's say you are making $25,000 a year, driving some old car, wearing worn clothes, living in a so-so apartment. You get a job advancement and a raise. What do you do? You do what everybody does; you buy a new car, new clothes, and other stuff. That's what we work for. However, it never stops. Most of us are never completely satisfied with what we have."

The comedian George Carlin had a line that is worth some thought: "Whoever dies with the most stuff wins."

My dad advised, "Save 10-20 percent of your income every week, month, and year. Put the cash in the bank first. After you have $1,000, invest in a very conservative instrument, maybe bonds or blue chip stocks."

My dad felt that living below your net income was very important, as did his parents. Saving while not going into debt was critical. He would profess to me, starting at the age of ten, "Tommy, cash is king. Having money available will free you from dependence on the government, your parents, or anyone. When you have money, banks will loan you more money against this cash and this is leverage. And leverage is what allows individuals to become wealthy."

As I got older and he felt I was ready for a more advanced education, he would expand his explanation: "Tom, when you get into the habit of saving and investing, it will continue your entire life. Good versus bad money management is what separates the economic classes in our country. Money reinvested will generally double every seven years. Therefore, your money is like working a second job with no effort. Plus, it works seven days a week, twenty-four hours a day. Whatever amount you set, stick with it. If it's 10 percent, never fall short. If you can stretch to 20 percent, your growth will be twice as fast. Saving must be a daily habit. Also, spending and going deeper into debt can easily be a habit—a bad habit but nonetheless a habit that most people fall into." Mr. Simmons loved to tell me, "The frugal man will never go broke." Starting back with the snow shoveling business, I followed this rule, which is the reason I graduated from high school with $6,500.

Most entrepreneurial quests will require your own money to get started. That's why saving and growing your hard-earned money is so critical.

22

Snap-A-Habit

"When dreams die, life is a broken-winged bird
that cannot fly."

—Langston Hughes (1902-1967),
American poet

My dad had a very inventive mind. As a marketing and advertising director, he was responsible for entertaining various clients, and he enjoyed an adult beverage or two. He also smoked. He never did it in our house because of my asthma, but when he was out entertaining or just with the boys, he lit up. He smoked Tareyton 100's, probably a bad one. He would tell me, "Quitting smoking is one of the easiest things I have ever done. In fact," he would go on, "I have done it many, many times; it's easy."

One of his friends who was trying to quit smoking told him that he wears a rubber band around his wrist to remind him to not smoke.

At lunch we talked about "inventing" the concept of wearing a rubber band around your wrist for this purpose. Whenever the urge to smoke a cigarette came to you, you should snap the band and pop yourself. My dad said, "This concept could apply to many other vices as well—drinking, gambling, eating too much, or anything else a person is trying to control." This conversation triggered my dad's artistic ability to come out again.

By our next lunch, our juices were flowing. He brought his sketch pad with a number of box designs. I wrote the instruction for its use and our idea took shape. He asked, "What do you think we should call this product?" I said, "Well, the idea is to snap yourself into remembering you want to quit your habit, right?" He agreed.

I said, "Why don't we call it Snap-A-Habit?" Dad loved the name.

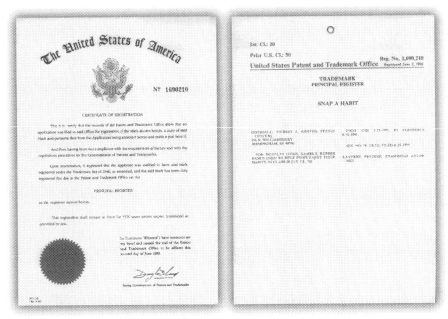

U.S. Patent 1992 for Snap-A-Habit

It's easy to come up with excuses for not accomplishing our goals, but that is the easy way out. An endless number of potential entrepreneurs ponder numerous ideas that never get off the ground. How many times have you said or heard someone say, "I had that same idea, and it should be me who is making all that money"?

The only difference is one person acted on the idea and pounded away. Don't fill your life with reasons for not starting or finishing something. Forget the excuse; forge ahead.

We worked on the design and development for Snap-A-Habit for two months. After a number of box designs, we settled on one. Then I found a graphic layout firm to do the box die and cutting. I also located a rubber-band manufacturing company. We decided pink was the right color. It would draw attention to the band and people who wore it would have to explain to those around them what they were attempting to quit. We figured others would reinforce and encourage the person who was wearing the band.

We even applied for and received a patent for the product from the U.S. Patent Office.

Snap-A-Habit box, 1992

I had big plans for our success, so I ordered 1,000 pink rubber bands with SNAP-A-HABIT printed on them. I was the marketing director for this product, appointed by my dad. He said, "This will be great experience for you. A big step up from the flyers you did for the snow and lawn maintenance business."

We decided the next step would be to write letters to large corporate marketing directors. I knew this would be another great learning experience, and I was game for the task. I wrote to fifty companies, from Wam-O to K-mart to Walmart, even to the American Cancer Society.

Rejection after rejection came our way. I called everyone we sent a letter to. Some sent a *nice* rejection letter; most never called back.

After a year of planning, designing, and marketing, we decided to scrap our project. We had a great time, and I learned a lot from the experience and the effort I put forward.

We figured we did everything we could to see our project through.

One year later, the Lance Armstrong Foundation came out with the yellow band for cancer awareness and research.

My family and everyone who knew about our Snap-A-Habit went crazy. All we needed was Lance Armstrong and we would have sold millions. It's funny, I still have all the rubber bands and packaging.

Though some might deem this whole venture a failure, it was not. We gained more than we lost. We had a great time planning and designing the product, then marketing and promoting it. Indeed, the gains from the experience were substantial.

23

Back to the Future

By fall 1987, my dad and I had been meeting for weekly lunch dates for four years. We finally decided it was time to try another restaurant for our Friday lunches, Tango's. It was also located at the Town Center, so we could both still walk to lunch.

At one of our lunches, I asked my dad, "Remember when I was living in the rental up at MSU with the Beal Street gang and I tried to talk you into buying a rental?" He did, and commented, "I'm glad I didn't go that route and buy one because I would be the one dealing with it today while you launched your career. Why do you ask?"

Twelve years after I tried to convince my dad to invest in rentals, I still felt it would be a promising investment. I told him I was going up to East Lansing to look at a property I knew was going on the market.

So I went and looked over the student rental. I had graduated ten years earlier, but I felt the campus and surrounding area had changed very little since that time. Most of the rentals looked the same as well—sort of shabby and in need of attention. Most of the houses near campus were built in the 1940s and 1950s, wooden two-story frame houses with four, five, or six bedrooms. Long ago, they had been converted to student-occupied rentals. Year in and year out, four to ten kids would live in each of these houses. Many off-campus college parties took place in these neighborhoods.

Imagine the fraternity parties, like those in the movie *Animal House*, going on most weekends. The rentals were well-worn but livable to college-age kids on their own for the first time.

My interest in looking at this house was strictly as an investor. I remember the lessons I learned from Mr. Williams:

- ROI (return on investment) must be greater than 15 percent.
- Cash flow has to be positive.
- Maintenance—make sure the house looks good, especially from the outside.

I knew location was everything, because I had been a student both on and off campus. I knew which locations would always be leased. With the right investment numbers, the only downside would be making sure it was always filled with renters.

After two trips up to East Lansing and the MSU area, I found a great house. It appraised for $5,000 more than the asking price. Back in those days, banks would make loans up to the appraisal value amount. So, at my very first closing, I purchased a rental and walked away with $5,000 in my pocket. I financed 100 percent of the purchase price and closing costs. No money down.

Although "no money down" is a thing of the past, there are still great ways to prosper in the real estate rental business. Study up, and make sure the following applies or don't buy it:

- Rent = X
- Expenses = Y
- Net = X-Y results in profit at least 10 percent of any investment. If it's greater, all the better.

The day you purchase a property is the day you make or lose money. That's because it's critical to know that you paid less than you can sell it for.

Such knowledge requires understanding the market. What are the current rents? How many tenants can you legally put into the property? What is the rating on a 0-5 desirability chart? In the college town where I owned houses, a "5" was for a house within four blocks of campus, near the bars, and close to the sorority houses. Boys love these houses and will even offer to pay more for a rental if they're competing with others for it. Watch out to see if there is rent control. If there isn't, it's a plus.

The way you also command more rent is by how the house looks inside and out. That's why Mr. Williams had his houses painted so often. First impressions are very important. The first thing a kid sees is the outside of the house, and many student houses look really bad—peeling paint and scruffy lawns. Also, usually at some point the students' parents will see the house and they can kill most rental opportunities without even entering the house.

In East Lansing, the city inspectors were hardest on the landlords with houses that looked bad. They inspected them once a year and would nickel-and-dime bad landlords.

On inspection day, I would always arrive early, waiting out in front of my rental, coffee and donut in hand for the inspector. After proving my houses were "clean" and up to code, the inspector eventually stopped bothering to go into the house. I would talk about sports or whatever for ten minutes in front of my house while he drank his coffee. Then he would get his clipboard out, fill out the approval paperwork, and sign it. He would give me my copy, return to his car, and be off.

Business was great; within six months of purchasing my first house, I purchased three more. I loved this "passive income," as my former mentor had called it. I was always looking for more properties and eventually owned fifteen rental houses.

I found the best time to approach a current owner is in the summer months. Most landlords hated this time, because kids would skip out on the rent. You might get three of the five kids paying.

They would forfeit the security deposit of one and a half months and then not pay two or three months and leave a few holes in the walls. I loved buying in the summer from frustrated single-property rental owners. Mr. Williams had told me this was when he purchased most of his rentals.

I learned who owned each property by utilizing public records. I came up with a process for my acquisitions: Pick the streets I wanted to potentially buy rentals on. Map it out with all the addresses: Beal 103-310, Grove 370-400, Ann 420-615, or Division 405-693. Then I would go to the city assessor's office and request information on the property I was interested in. The city is required to provide a public record of tax payers.

The first time the clerk told me she wouldn't do all that work. However, by law, she had to allow me access to the information. So she let me go through all the files and pick out the information I wanted. I could also see which properties were in tax default, another great buying opportunity. After going in again and again, the clerk would share inside information with me as well—troubled properties, etc., again great buying opportunities. I didn't do anything crazy to get this information. Kindness was all it took.

Today, with computers, this process would be a lot easier. Back then, I sat for hours writing down each address and the taxpayer of record. For example:

515 Ann Street property owner: Bill Smith
123 Main Street
Rochester, MI 48120
Phone: 248-555-1234

I discovered that this market was very fragmented. A few landlords owned more than twenty rentals. Mr. Williams now had forty-three rentals; however, the majority only owned one or two. They were my target. I wrote every one of these owners a letter.

GOTSHALL PROPERTIES

April 23, 1989

Mr. Joe Walker
456 Main Street
Lansing Michigan
Dear Mr. Walker;

Currently I'm in the process of purchasing student rental properties in East Lansing Michigan. In my investigation I have discovered you own a rental at 504 MAC Ave. I own a few properties in the area and I would be interested in discussing the prospects of purchasing your rental if you are interested.

My process would be to meet you at the rental property, have it inspected by a licensed inspector. I would also check with the city and make sure it is licensed as a rental property, and all corresponding fees are paid and current.

This process would take five to ten days. If at the conclusion of this process we could settle on a price. I would be prepared to close within two weeks for cash.

I'm a qualified and serious buyer and I hope to purchase five properties within the next four weeks. I also have my real-estate license and we could complete the transaction without a broker which would save you the real-estate commission.

If you are interested please contact me at 517-555-1234.

Sincerely;

Thomas Gotshall

I figured, if they were thinking about selling, why not cut out the real estate sales commission of 6-8 percent?

The key was I had my purchasing formula.

I sent out fifty letters each week, starting with my number one areas. After three days, I would call the owner, always after 7 p.m., post dinner, and before 9:30 p.m. I would keep track of all the unanswered calls. After a total of five times, I would remove them from the list.

I had many fascinating discussions. Many of these houses were the rentals that were in the best condition in the area, and I often found that these owners wanted out, sooner versus later.

Also of public record was when the house last sold and at what price—critical information.

Out of each batch of fifty, I would usually get five to seven landlords who were interested in selling.

Time was on my side, and the buyer is in control. This was business, no emotional component. If someone would tell me they had many people who were interested in purchasing their great property, I would respond, "Sounds like you have a few sales opportunities already lined up. If they fall through, give me a call." In reality, the seller usually didn't have someone hot to buy, or they wouldn't have talked to me in the first place.

My goal was to buy low. However, if my offer was too much of a "low ball," sometimes they would never contact me again. But I could make a few unhappy and still have a massive inventory to pick from, and besides, by selling to me, they didn't have to list the house and pay real estate commission. Also, I was preapproved by my bank and had the ability to close in five days, very appealing to the anxious seller.

I got to know the other major players to the market. Whenever I was in East Lansing, which was seventy miles from my home, I would make it a point to grab coffee and lunch with one of them. They had a vast amount of helpful information to share and, as always, I was good at listening.

I knew one owner had most of the houses on a section of Charles Street. One summer, I purchased a house on Charles for $65,000, raised the rent for the incoming fall group, and spent $600 to have it painted. Then I called that guy and sold the house to him for $82,500. I had owned that house for less than thirty days.

Here's how the transaction went down:

Selling price $82,500
Return on investment (ROI)
Net $16,900 in thirty days
$16,900 / $65,600 = 25%

This was grand. I loved the business. Still, things change and a successful entrepreneur knows that you can't get attached to any one strategy or opportunity.

As with the snow shoveling and house painting businesses, this venture required many hours and hard work. These hours were in addition to those I put into my full-time job selling computers. Most of the time I spent attending to the rental business was in the evening and on weekends, though the advent of cell phones made it easy to be available when needed.

I'm not a fix-it-up type of guy, so I hired a maintenance company to do all the repairs on my rentals. Plus, I had a painting crew for the summer. And I happened to have a cousin attending MSU, so Mark Sassack became my rent collector.

When my new tenants moved in, I was there to greet them. I would provide monthly payment envelopes as well as my cell phone number and that of my collections manager, Mark. I explained that I had attended MSU. That, plus the fact that I was only seven or eight years older than my tenants, contributed to an easygoing relationship with the renters.

I would pick a "captain" for each rental and ask that person to be the point person to communicate any problems to me. I would give tenants a twelve-pack of beer, if they were of age, and hand $20 to the captain. I would usually pull this person aside and explain that if there weren't any problems and I received all the rent on time, I would pay him or her $50 at the conclusion of the lease. For the typical lease of $1,200 a month, this was nothing.

My student rental business was in full swing. I formed Gotshall Properties and was earning pre-tax revenue of $60,000 to $90,000 each year. Then things took a very bad turn.

Each rental property had a tenant rating that specified how many people were allowed to live there; often it had nothing to do with the size or even number of bedrooms of the rental. I owned a house on MAC Avenue with seven bedrooms and a rating of four tenants. About 95 percent of the student rentals had one, two, or three more kids than the rating allowed. Although this benefitted the landlords, it mostly helped out the kids. The economy would allow rent of $1,400 a month. With seven bedrooms, this meant each tenant paid $200 a month; if there were only four tenants, the rent would be $350 each.

I will admit that some rentals jammed kids in over the reasonable limit. Some would allow ten kids in a house with just five bedrooms. I argued with the City Inspector the number of bedrooms should equal the number of tenants, excluding basements and attics if two exits didn't exist. But logic seemed to not apply to the city's rating system.

In the spring of 1991, tragedy struck. At a big house party at one of the rental houses in town, a student passed out in the attic and died when the house caught fire. The landlord of this house owned just two houses.

Terrible for everyone involved, mostly the family of the dead college student. Send your son or daughter off to college to get an education and they never come home.

Well the crap hit the fan for landlords. Every inspector made "surprise" inspections the following week. Citations and lawsuits were everywhere. The big owners were hit the hardest.

I was no exception. My seven-bedroom house on MAC got busted. Seven kids in a house rated for four. The house was huge—twelve could have lived in the house.

The *Lansing State Journal* was hot for a story. They followed around an inspector, and at my MAC house, he knocked and went in. Wouldn't you know, every kid was home. The inspector said, "We are from the city and we want to just look around: seven bedrooms, seven kids. Next the reporter from the paper comes in. Now the boys are drawn by this—*Wow, the newspaper!*

They interview them, and then they say, "How about a picture?" In front of the house they have three of them sit on the street corner and take their picture.

The next day, the paper's front-page headline announced, "Crowded Out" and three kids were forced to move out.

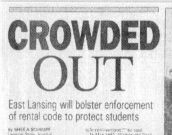

ticketed the landlord, and three tenants — two living in the attic and one in the basement — moved out.

Landlord Tom Gotshall, a 1978 MSU graduate, paid the $250 fine on March 1.

"It has reshaped my thinking a bit," said Gotshall, who owns six student rentals. He plans to own 20 or 30 houses some day.

His tenants say that as many as 80 or 90 percent of the houses in the immediate neighborhood are overoccupied.

"I don't want to chug to class all winter. You must make concessions," said Tim Conroy, an accounting major from Flint.

Gotshall said the demand for prime locations is so high he has already rented the house to five students for fall.

"The guys line up," he said.

Houses stuffed beyond the legal limit both cause and result from inflated housing prices.

Some landlords set rent higher because they know they will rent to more than the limit, Thomas said. Students look at high rent and immediately look for an extra tenant to share the load.

Thomas thinks rents will go down if overoccupancy is reduced. Students will probably not pay $300 or more a month in rent, so landlords will be forced to charge less.

But several landlords agreed that rents will never go down. Rent of $300 a month compares with the $326 or so students pay for room and board in a residence hall.

"Parents are paying the bills," said George Danford, who owns 25 rental properties. "I don't get any checks from students. All my checks are from Birmingham and Bloomfield Hills."

Danford said students often slip in without notifying the landlord.

"The city of East Lansing cannot employ enough people to baby-sit all the houses in East Lansing," he said.

Bob Metzger, who owns more

Upcoming hearings

These hearings are scheduled on proposed rental code revisions:

■ A public hearing on new regulations for rubbish, nuisances and litter, April 3

■ A Housing Commission public hearing on the main revisions, April 19

than 40 rental units, said landlords have to recoup losses they suffer in summer when tenants skip out on leases.

Metzger and Gotshall said overoccupancy was a bigger problem about 10 years ago.

"I lived in a house where we had twice as many people as we were supposed to," Gotshall said.

Overcrowding may not be a universal problem in college towns.

Jack Donaldson, Ann Arbor housing director, said cases of University of Michigan students sleeping in attics, closets and basements are not frequent.

He said he could not recall a student dying because of inadequate exits or illegal occupancy.

Ann Arbor inspects and recertifies its 24,000 rental units every 30 months, basing the occupancy limits on the number and size of sleeping areas. The city also has nuisance codes that govern the appearance and upkeep of properties.

East Lansing, with a population of about 50,000, has about 28,000 student tenants.

The city issued 1,523 licenses for rental property in the past year. Each property is inspected annually, and licensing limits are set by zoning, number of exits, width of stairways and parking.

Besides overoccupancy tickets,

the city issued 69 tickets for various violations, Thomas said.

Student tenants and permanent residents conflict in many ways, Thomas said. Tenants on their own for the first time are inclined to do things they have never been allowed to do at home.

Neighbors complain of noise, off-street parking and trash. Many of the code revisions are designed to reduce friction between the two groups, stop blight, and slow conversions of owner-occupied houses to rentals.

"It's a three-party constituency, a balancing act," Thomas said, "the landlord, the tenant and the neighborhood."

The new code will allow landlords to use leases that make tenants responsible for shoveling snow and cutting grass. Landlords still will be responsible for major items such as furnaces, Thomas said.

The property owner or a legal representative must appear in person when applying for a rental license and supply a street address rather than a post office box.

The proposed code revisions were a compromise, Housing Commission Chair Judy Karandjeff said. "Nobody was totally happy."

The 142-page proposed code should reduce confusion by pulling together ordinances and putting them in clearer language, she said.

"East Lansing is going to a higher standard," said Rose Norwood, director of the Housing Resource Center, a non-profit counseling agency.

"The city has always had ordinances, but the code strengthens them and makes tenants responsible for violations."

Darin Lounds, a student board chair in the Associated Students of MSU, said overoccupancy was not a choice students eagerly make.

"No one wants to be overcrowded. But what are you going to do?"

Crackdown on cramped rentals

By Sheila Schimpf
Gannett News Service

EAST LANSING — East Lansing is cracking down on hundreds of Michigan State University students who sleep cramped into attics, coal bins and closets in rent-splitting schemes.

City Housing Director Nick Thomas, fearing fire deaths, vowed increased enforcement of the city's housing code and stiffer penalties for landlords who let students live in one-exit areas that fail standards for human habitation.

Thomas is working with the Housing Commission and a citizens' task force to revise the housing code.

In May 1987, 23-year-old Paul Charles died in a fire in a rental house licensed for eight. He was asleep in a closet and was overcome by smoke.

"How can I protect them if I don't know they're living in an unsafe environment?" Thomas asked.

His major weapon will be a ticket for overoccupancy. In the last 12 months, the city issued only 18 such tickets, down from 21 in 1986.

"It's going to happen more," said Thomas, who plans to recommend that the base fine be raised from $250 to $500.

Tom Gotshall, a 1978 MSU graduate, paid a $250 fine this month for allowing eight men to live in a house licensed for five. They paid $185

apiece for the monthly rent.

"It has reshaped my thinking a bit," said Gotshall, who owns six student rentals.

Gotshall said the demand for prime locations is so high "the guys line up" when the apartment becomes available and are willing to endure cramped conditions to be close to the campus and have a reasonable monthly rent.

East Lansing — with a population of about 50,000 — has about 28,000 student tenants.

The city issued 1,523 licenses for rental property in the last year. Each property is inspected annually and licensing limits are set by zoning, number of exits, width of stairways and parking.

East Lansing Journal article, March 1991

Also that day a reporter calls me with "just a few questions." Now I have great respect for the media. My dad worked at two different newspapers before working for the U.S. Chamber of Commerce. However, when they want to go negative, my advice is don't grant an interview.

I got smeared in the interview. "Out-of-town land barren grants overcrowding in his slums." For the next week the inspectors were everywhere. The heat was on them big time, and so they cracked down on us landlords everywhere they could.

However, within a month it was business as usual.

I somehow found a place for my three evicted students for a little while. The problem I had now wasn't the City of East Lansing inspectors, it was the federal government. Housing violations fall under HUD, which can become federal lawsuits with potential jail time attached to them.

The Associated Press wire service picked up the story, and the *Detroit Free Press*—one of the newspapers my dad had worked for in his early years—and the *Detroit News* picked up and ran the story.

Great, all kinds of people called me, including my father, father-in-law, and boss.

My dad: "Never be interviewed on a negative story."

My father-in-law: "Don't drag my daughter into this crazy mess."

My boss: "What the hell's going on? How can you own rentals at MSU?"

Every entrepreneur encounters an unknown variety of issues and problems; anticipate them in your planning. When I was shoveling snow and it turned to ice, I used rock salt to thaw the ice. When it rained while I was painting rentals, we would spend the day scraping future houses so we wouldn't get behind. I knew about making the best of a bad situation, but this one threw me for a loop.

When a major unknown comes your way, evaluate all aspects, improvise, adjust your plan, make a short/long-term decision, and execute the plan.

24

Passive Income

"My father was an amazing man. The older I got,
the smarter he got."

—Mark Twain (1835-1910),
American author

I remember quite clearly having lunch with my dad in 1991 after all of these problems developed with my rental business. I questioned, "What—my rental on MAC got busted?" I was frustrated and a little freaked out, which of course my dad knew right away.

I started, "What in the world should I do with this major mess on my hands?" He responded, "Calm down and first deal with the problem in front of you. Hire a local well-respected lawyer and do it today. Follow his lead and do the right thing. Don't cut any corners and take your medicine. Next, reevaluate your business plan. Do you want to continue with this project, or could it be the right time to launch your next enterprise?"

Now back to 1991, I was strongly considering quitting my job and starting my own computer company or even something else. Maybe the rental property problem was just the push I needed. My dad often would say, "There is no such thing as problems, only opportunities."

Three weeks after the picture in the journal, I had hired the number one real estate attorney in East Lansing, a friend of the judge. I ended up paying out $10,000 in legal fees, plus a small fine of $1,500, and then I walked.

Next, after careful planning, I decided I would sell all my rentals. The money from the sales would provide the necessary starting cash to launch my computer company.

I knew the top six rental property owners in East Lansing. Over the years, I had coffee, lunch, and a few drinks with all of them. I created a spreadsheet detailing my properties, including rent, expenses, taxes, and asking price. Now I was a seller, not a buyer. I had been very selective with my purchasing and consequently had properties in some of the best rental locations in town. Also, I maintained my properties very well. They all had fresh paint on them, new appliances, and were cleaner than most rentals.

My first call was to Mr. Williams. "Hello Mr. Williams," I said. "I have decided to sell my rentals and I wanted to give you first crack at them. I would be happy to send you a list of them with all the pertinent information: addresses, current rent, taxes, maintenance cost, and records for the past twelve months."

Mr. Williams said, "Has the city busted your balls to the extent that you have had enough? I hope it's not just that. Things will settle down soon and be back to 'normal.' You are a good landlord and should stick with it. Besides who am I going to share war stories with?"

I responded, "My approval with the city is no big deal to me. I've decided to start a new venture, and I need to slowly sell my rental investments for the liquidity. I have enjoyed the rental business, but now is the time for me to move on."

He asked me to send the list and said he would let me know.

My plan was to first contact all the major players in the marketplace and try to sell all the properties to them. After that, I would consider listing the rentals with a real estate broker and pay the commission.

I also set a fair but profitable price on each property and said the selling price was firm. Period. Always make a strong stand. If I would have said, "I'm negotiable or shoot me an offer," every one of these professional rental properties owners would have figured the starting price was 10-15 percent less than my published price.

I also had all of my properties inspected and a report prepared. Everyone knew the inspection company I selected and most used the same one themselves, so they knew the inspection would be spot-on. In addition, I had signed leases for the upcoming fall term. It was really a numbers game. We all used the same ROI metrics, and though my prices were a little high, based on location, all were good buys.

The first house I sold was MAC, the one in the news story. The reason, best location right next to a large sorority house; plus MAC is the center of rental row, close to campus and the bars. I had purchased the house for $85,000, and four years later sold it for $115,000.

I had financed this house with $15,000 cash down. It was a sound investment. My annual net profit from it after mortgage, taxes, insurance, and maintenance was $4,950.

The total picture of the numbers looked like this:

$115,000 selling
$65,000 bank payoff ($85,000 less $20,000 for the down payment and mortgage)
$50,000 cash at closing back to me

$19,500 rent net income for four years
$69,500 total income ($50,000 plus $19,500)
$15,000 down payment when I purchased

Return on investment (ROI)
$ 69,500 / $ 20,000 = 347 %

Not bad for passive income.

As it turned out, I sold every one of my houses to my target audience within three weeks.

I enjoyed the whole experience of buying, owning, operating, and finally selling student rental properties. I learned an endless array of things about both business and dealing with people.

Here is my take-away from the experience: Seek out the experts and "pick their brains." You must earn this right, so put in your work. Ask a lot of questions and shut up.

Study the marketplace: I knew the MSU campus and surrounding area. Stay with what you know. In real estate, location is everything. A property within walking distance of campus would earn 50-100 percent more rent and selling price than a comparable rental twenty minutes away.

Hire the best professionals to fill critical roles. I hired the services of two great real estate attorneys in town. They knew the laws and judges and, yes, I knew about the housing ratings. Don't cut corners or try and fill a role you are not trained to do. From attorney to accountants to even maintenance companies, get the job done right the first time and hire the best.

Know the numbers: The goal is to make money, so it is important to understand all aspects of your business. In this case, rent, expenses, mortgage, and anything that will affect your profit margin. Have a rainy day fund for unexpected stuff.

Also closely check out all your potential tenants. And finally keep your eye on the ball. Stay involved and informed with all aspects of your business.

25

Valley and Mountain People

A few weeks after I sold all my rental properties, my dad and I both knew I was getting closer to my next entrepreneurial endeavor—starting another business. I remember my dad telling me this during lunch one day:

> There are two types of people in the world, especially in the sales profession and the entrepreneurial game. They are valley people and mountain people.
>
> You can reside in the valley. Those types of people are usually very critical and negative. Their first thought is to blame someone or something for what is wrong with any situation.
>
> Or you can stand proud on the mountaintop. These types of people are positive, energetic, and always pushing for results. They never look to blame others. Whatever situation they are presented with is an opportunity to excel and make a difference.
>
> Occasionally a valley person will make a run up the mountain. However, if any little "slips" comes along, back down they slide to the valley because it's easier.
>
> Sure, they'll poke at everything. But when the adversity comes and the water streams down the hill and forms a river, they will be washed away, into the ocean of Loser Ville.

I laughed at my dad's crazy analogy. However, I thought about some of the successful people I had worked with over the years. Fred Hill and Mr. Williams, they were mountain people—successful, positive, and pushing for results. I knew I wanted to be on that same mountaintop.

So in 1992, it was finally the right time to dedicate myself full time to my entrepreneurial quest. I decided to apply everything I had learned up until now and just go for it. Among the lessons I had learned:

1. From asthma, I learned how to cope with something I had no control over.
2. The snow shoveling and lawn maintenance business taught me how to recognize a need (snow removal, spring and fall cleanup, and mowing), provide a service at a fair price, over-serve the client, and go the extra mile to build reoccurring revenue.
3. My rental house painting business taught me to look at the big picture (thirty-two houses in need of painting), build a business plan capable of solving the problem, and hire the necessary help and manage them as a team. When obstacles arise (rain or going back to school), I learned to modify the plan, improvise, and conquer.
4. I learned even more from owning rental properties: build a business model, evaluate the market, and develop a method for acquiring property. Apply a proven ROI methodology, negotiate hard when you are the buyer, and hold firm when you are the seller. I also learned the importance of surrounding yourself with top-notch professionals.
5. A unique prospective and a positive attitude are critical outlooks.

I learned another lesson from up on the mountain. Other positive individuals are also up there and they are the best people to be associated with. Plus the view is better and you can see much further ahead than the rest of the world, especially all those valley people.

26

Pursuing the American Dream

"Becoming an entrepreneurial genius isn't an overnight sensation. It takes time and persistence."
—Robert H. Gotshall Sr. (1927-2004),
father and teacher

It was 1992 and my dad and I had been meeting for lunch on Fridays for ten years by now. We had covered an endless number of topics, ranging from marriage and raising kids to building friendships and trust to handling jobs and bosses. But mostly, we talked about the American dream: creating wealth and becoming an entrepreneur. I was ready to pursue my entrepreneurial vision. The only problem was, I didn't have the concept yet.

At lunch I said, "Dad, I know now is the time for me to go off and start something. The only problem is, I'm not really sure just what to start." I thought he would tell me this sounded crazy. You want to break out and pursue the American dream of starting a business, but you just don't know what it should be?

Instead, what my dad said was brilliant: "Makes sense to me. After all those years of having a business of your own—the snow shoveling and lawn maintenance business, then the campus painting business, and finally the rental business—and after working for GM and finally two computer companies, MAI and ComputerVision, you realize your true passion was always creating and running your own business. You, my boy, are a true entrepreneur. You know your destiny; now you only need to look at the world and decide just what entrepreneurial direction to take. Simple."

He went on, "You should stick with something you know. Many people make the mistake of venturing into something they know very little about and then falling fast and hard on their face."

I said, "Well, that makes sense. I'm sure there is an opportunity to start a snow removal and lawn maintenance, residential, or even commercial venture. However, been there, done that. The house painting business was great but too much manual labor. The rental business was interesting. However, I felt I lacked the passion for it. The computer business is growing and changing every day. I understand the industry and am passionate about the sales, marketing, and financial possibilities. However, I am not a super geek." For the next few months, we talked about the computer industry plus all the other aspects of funding, starting, and running a business.

In the 1990s, the computer industry was changing the way end users could purchase hardware, software, and services. In the "old days," an end user dealt directly with the manufacturer. So, for example, if an organization wanted to buy an IBM server, they purchased it from IBM directly. Same with HP, Sun Microsystems, Oracle, and Dell.

In fact, this was true of all computer companies. But now the industry was starting to shift to an indirect purchasing model. First, the small players, then finally the big companies began to license resellers to market, sell, install, and service all their products and manage the relationship with the end user. Manufacturers provided a greater margin to the reseller, and they made a nice profit after setting a higher price for the end user. Also, in the beginning, resellers were only allowed to manage small- and medium-size accounts. I was watching this development with great interest. And luck was on my side.

I was still a sales executive at ComputerVision and managing about forty accounts. I had started at the company in November 1988. The management of ComputerVision called a company-wide meeting in December 1991. Whenever they did this, it meant some big announcement was coming, and it was usually bad. It was set up as a teleconference with all the offices online, including those in North America, Europe, and Asia.

At the meeting, they announced the formation of the reseller channel for the entire company. The newly named director talked about the need to embrace the new strategy of selling our products through an independent body of companies. The resellers would deal with the smaller companies, and we would concentrate on the larger companies. This strategy would allow the overall corporation to grow and prosper. As a publicly traded stock, we needed to make this move. It was very important and was all good.

However, now came the other news: "Our new direction needs a kick start. Therefore, all of you will be asked to turn over 40 percent of your existing customers to the newly signed resellers. You'll need to meet with your sales manager and identify these accounts within the next two weeks." Nobody was happy with this corporate dictate, except maybe me. After the call ended, everybody simultaneously went crazy. The collective cry was, "Are you kidding? How can they demand we turn over 40 percent of our accounts and income? Those bastards!"

Just before the meeting in our office concluded, our sales manager, Sam Lawrence, asked, "Other than bitching, do any of you have any questions?" I said, "As you would expect, none of us are real happy about this. However, I do have a question. Just who are the resellers in our area of Michigan?" Sam replied, "We will tell you just who they are in a few weeks." So off we went. Over the next few weeks, we all put together our account lists and waited for the announcement of the resellers.

27

The Start of an Idea

I could not wait for the next lunch with my dad, so I could tell him of the latest development at ComputerVision. When we met, I told him what had happened and questioned whether I should throw my hat in the ring now and start my company before it was too late. He advised me to wait and see who they anointed as the resellers before I made a move. He felt that since the announcement was coming within a few weeks, the company had already selected the resellers and I should wait and see what things looked like after the announcement.

Two weeks later ComputerVision announced the names of the new resellers. Both were small firms that had zero experience with our products and services. This made all the sales executives even madder. "How could they turn over our accounts to inexperienced computer resellers?" Again, more good news from my perspective as I shifted into entrepreneurial creation.

After all the years of both pursuing entrepreneurial ventures and talking and talking about all the aspects of business—from concept, goals, missions, along with financing and running it—the brain power required to actually conceive and plan my next company, Technical Solutions, Inc. (TSI), was easy. In fact, the concept for Technical Solutions was conceived on a bar napkin.

Original business plan and logo
for Technical Solutions, Inc., 1992

I bet many great entrepreneurial ideas are born in this fashion. I was antsy to launch a business in the computer industry and seized the opportunities that existed with the shift occurring in the way the manufacturers interacted with customers. The introduction of value-added resellers was a real plus in my eyes.

I will not get into a long description of this industry. The short explanation is as follows: Every computer installation has a number of different computer components as part of the solution. They are purchased from original equipment manufacturers (OEMs). An installation may consist of servers from IBM, storage from Hitachi, database software from Oracle, security products from Symantic, routers and switches from Cisco, and finally, the application software from a variety of companies.

For the end user, this can be, and usually is, a nightmare—coordinating all the different and sometimes competing organizations that must work together to achieve the desired solution.

As a sales executive representing one of the pieces of the puzzle, I was well aware of all the issues in this process. Company A blaming company B for issues. Or company C not delivering at the target installation date and blowing the crossover from the old system to the new and blaming the other company's computer operation and temporarily making the IT staff look really bad.

My idea for TSI was to be the glue to bring the complete solution together for the end user. This was better for the end user because he or she would have one coordinated installation by one organization, the reseller. Instead of trying to deal with three or four different OEMs, we could offer a turnkey bundle, including hardware, software, maintenance, and support.

Today, almost every OEM conducts 60-80 percent of its business through resellers. The OEM provides a reseller with 15-50 percent in margin and lets the seller negotiate with the end user and make what it can.

I felt uniquely positioned to provide this service and was anxious to launch TSI. Mark Oakes, my technology associate where I worked, and I went out to a bar. I took a bar napkin out and wrote down the business concept in seven bullet points. And we talked through them all.

That same night I settled on the company name, Technical Solutions, Inc., and Mark designed the logo. I felt our company name should tell it all. We would provide technology packages that are complete solutions, making Technical Solutions our name an easy choice. We did this all in a few hours. It should be noted that naming your company is very important. It becomes your brand and you do not want to change it. Also don't get too cute or flip with your name. Once you settle on the name go online to your state government website and see if your chosen name is available for incorporating. If it is available grab it along with names that are similar. The same holds true for registering it as a website.

The next day I wrote out the needs and solution matrix, and it was that simple. The business plan was more complex to develop and took more thought and time. But we were off to a good start.

The needs and solution matrix was two columns of information. The first column lists ten different computer needs a typical end user might have. In the next column, 1A, was the solution that we would offer. As an example, our first listed need was:

1. Turnkey engineering workstation with CV software
1. A. Sun Micro solutions or H/P workstation, bundled with the required software

The second need was installation.
2. Installation onsite of the workstation and software
2. A. For $200 per workstation, we would provide onsite installation and networking

This is the beginning of building your company offering. This will also become part of your business plan later.

28

My Supportive Wife, Marti

All my years of lunch with Dad were always wonderful. They would last one to two hours and we were always surprised at how the time would seem to fly by. However, now our lunches were business and planning meetings. Looking back, I loved these lunches the most.

My dad started out at one lunch: "How does Marti feel about your idea of pulling the plug on your secure job, which includes a great salary, bonus, health care, and other benefits and rolling the bones?" My dad knew there was a lot of risk starting a company. Plus, if a spouse doesn't completely support the event, it would spell death for most dreaming entrepreneurs.

I told him, "Marti and I have talked about this potential day coming for a long time. She gets it! Plus, she knows that if I don't launch a full-time business venture, I'd probably regret it for the rest of my life."

I continued, "She is conservative and concerned; however, she trusts that I know just what I'm doing. Her positive spin is, 'If this doesn't work out, we can start over.' We started our marriage with less than $5,000 in the bank. And today I have a lot more going for myself—a great reputation and experience in the computer industry."

I knew this part of the equation was a must. Without the support of a spouse, most, if not all, entrepreneurs' ideas remain just that— ideas that never materialize.

Photo of Marti and me, Christmas 2002

THE DAREDEVIL ENTREPRENEUR

I spent six months putting my business plan for TSI together, before I quit my job. I knew my strengths: sales, marketing, plus administration along with financial record-keeping. I also knew my weakness: I was not a strong computer technician. So I had to convince the very best technical support person to join me. I turned again to my colleague Mark Oakes. His wife, Alice, freaked out. She was worried about their future, so I sat down with both of them over dinner to explore the possibilities. His concern was income and health care. I asked, "Anything else?" Nope.

I replied by saying I would guarantee his salary for two years plus a 10 percent increase. Also, I pledged that within a year I would vest (give) Mark stock in the company. I was not going to leave dinner that evening without Alice saying yes. After three hours of discussing it, both she and Mark agreed that he would join my new company.

Within one year I vested Mark with a 10 percent share of the company, plus a raise. His vesting required zero cash investment on his part. Over the eighteen years he stayed with the company, he made more money than he ever would have in corporate America. And when I eventually sold the company, he received a big fat check. But I know that without him, it would have been much more difficult to run TSI. I always told Mark that he was worth his weight in gold.

It is never completely the right time to make a leap. However, the circumstances were all lining up for me. The computer model was changing, and I had the necessary capital to launch my company from selling my rentals. Plus I felt in my soul that now was the time for me. Even so, I had two young kids (still one to follow), a mortgage, and all the expenses families have. I did not make this decision overnight.

My wife, Marti, always knew I had the burning drive inside of me to do this, and she trusted I could make it work. "If it all blows up, we start over. You could go back and find another computer sales position." She was right; I had worked hard and had a good reputation in the industry.

My dad's advice: "If you don't give it a real chance and go for it, you will always wonder if you could have made it." Deep down I knew my dad had always wished he, too, would have given it a try.

I had the confidence in myself from all of my earlier entrepreneurial experiences. I would work hard and be very persistent. We all know the naturally athletic person who excels at every sport or the really smart kid who never studies and gets all A's. I was not that kid. And that was an advantage, because I had learned from endless hard work that I could accomplish anything I set out to do. My experiences up to this point had taught me some elements very critical to success—discipline and the importance of a positive attitude.

As author and speaker Zig Ziglar says, "The most important word in the English language is *Attitude*. Having a great attitude will allow a person to overcome any adversity that comes his or her way."

29

A Moral Victory?

"A genius is a person who aims at something no one else can see and hits it."

—Ervin L. Glaspy

After I left MAI and joined ComputerVision, my dad and I decided to pick a third location for our lunch dates. We settled on Peabody's in downtown Birmingham. It's a perfect restaurant. Mr. Peabody started it in 1946, and for the most part, his three daughters were running it now. I think they have the best Manhattan clam chowder and Reuben sandwich in the world.

We always sat in the bar area where they had TVs broadcasting sports and Fox news. While we usually met for lunch on Fridays, we agreed to meet one Sunday in the fall because it was crunch time for the planning of TSI.

My dad loved watching sports: golf, football, baseball, and hockey. We were watching a football game that day between the Detroit Lions and the Chicago Bears. The Bears were favored by fourteen points. The Lions fought a great battle but lost in the last three seconds by a field goal. The announcers said a number of typical things and finished by saying it was a "moral victory" for the Lions!

"Moral victory—*are you kidding?*"

My dad yelled at the TV and proclaimed, "There is no such thing as a moral victory when you still lose in the end!"

So we talked about the so-called moral victory. My dad was crystal clear. Either you win or you lose, simple. That is the great thing about sports. There is a beginning and an end, one winner and one loser.

If you are there to compete, you only want to be the winner. You have to "lace them up" and go at it full force to win.

And don't stop until the final bell rings. Dad was on a roll.

He asked if I could feed my family with *moral victories*. Would I keep my job, with *moral victories*? Would I be a successful entrepreneur with *moral victories*?

No, on all accounts; point made.

Ask any competitive person after a loss if they feel good about their "moral victory."

The same holds true for me as an entrepreneur. I often reflected on Dad's "Moral Victory" philosophy as I began and started to build Technical Solutions. If I failed, there would be no sense of a moral victory.

The company would either succeed and exist or fail. If I failed, he was correct that I would not feel I had a "moral victory" just because I started a company that failed in the end.

Success for an entrepreneur can be many different things. For me, I felt success would be defined by the following list:

1. Starting and growing the company for over ten years. Over 97 percent of start-ups fail in the first three years. Our company TSI lasted over eighteen years.
2. Make a profit within one year. We were able to make a profit within our first full quarter, and we were profitable most every quarter we were in business.

3. Add one or two employees each year. We hired our first employee, Brian Lanfear, after being in business for four months. Every year thereafter we added employees, and in 2001 we hired fifteen new employees.
4. Become cash flow positive after three years. We became cash flow positive during our third year and remained so for many years.
5. Build up a line of credit of $2 million within three years. Our line grew to $5 million and we used very little of it.
6. Have a stable employee base with little turnover. Our average employee was with us for over seven years and we had ten employees who were with us for over twelve years and one for sixteen years.
7. Be respected in the local community and contribute to a number of charities. Our employees drove all this activity and we were very involved in Make a Wish Foundation, Susan G. Komen Breast Cancer drives and Cell Phones for Soldiers to name just a few.
8. Build and create wealth. Mission accomplished for many of us.

Before you start your entrepreneurial quest, you should create your own detailed list of what success would look like. Think short and long term, plus small and big picture. This will be your measuring stick and grading scale. Review it often and be truthful when grading your company.

30

In the Beginning

Any entrepreneurial endeavor requires planning, and then more planning. You will envision just what it will feel and look like in the beginning. If you are like most, you will think about this night and day. Even so, when the day arrives you will probably feel unprepared and nervous. Somehow many self-doubts will still enter your mind: *Have I thought of everything? Is this a major mistake? Is the timing right? What if I run out of money? Just what will others think?* On and on you will beat yourself up.

Normal, but shake it off and move forward.

Before resigning from ComputerVision, I wanted to have my business plan for TSI complete and the bank financing in place. Seven out of ten businesses fail in the first year due to poor cash flow (or available cash). In the second and third years, two of the remaining three fail because of, again, poor cash flow. Profits are very important. However, if you can't pay your employees, suppliers, rent, and other expenses, you are dead in the water.

I took my business plan to ten different banks and they all agreed that I had a sound and interesting plan. However, not one of them would give me a loan. The reason I got again and again was, we were not a proven entity, and they didn't want to take the risk. Banks are not in the business of taking risks. They will only loan money to a proven individual with a proven track record. In the end, I had to decide whether I was willing to invest my lifetime savings along with the profits from selling my fifteen rental properties. I felt my business plan was solid, so I made the hard decision to go forward and invest it all. From the start, TSI made money and grew each quarter. However, I would find myself telling my accountant, "Man, we are cooking with gas, profits are up, and I feel great. However, I don't have any cash—none, nada, zip."

He explained this was simply the dynamics of growth. It will take all your cash in the beginning to fuel your operation. In fact, I didn't have cash to put my hands on until year three.

On August 10, 1992, Mark and I resigned our positions and walked out. As the news spread among our former co-workers, they all said the same collective thing: We were nuts and would never last one month. Also, they figured we had no idea how to build and run a company. They thought we would be back, begging for our old jobs. The funny twist to this is, over the next few years many of these doubters came to us and asked for jobs.

In 1992, Mark and I rented two small offices in a "shared office" complex. The first day we bought two computers and ordered our business cards. We were both very excited and ready for whatever challenge came our way. We also ordered letterhead with our logo printed on it. The first order of business was to write a press release announcing the formation of TSI and then send it to all of our prospective accounts. After that, we started calling all these potential customers. My approach was to ask for a fifteen-minute meeting to explain our *value proposition*. I had a lot of sales experience, so this cold calling was right up my alley. Some accounts were willing to listen to us; most were "just too busy" now, but maybe they would have some time next month. This is just part of the game. The key is to get organized and keep calling and calling . . . and calling. In the first month, we went on many calls with no real results.

However, because we knew how the business worked, we were not discouraged. Most sales cycles in the computer business will take three to six months to get traction. It is a numbers game. You first build your prospective base and work it. We needed twenty active accounts at any given time to feel we were on track.

As a deal began to take shape, we needed to add another new opportunity into our pipeline. This holds true for most sales processes.

Our objective from the very beginning was for each sales executive, including me, to have the following at all times:

- 20 prospects
- 15 active deals
- 10 current proposals
- 5 pending decisions

Though the exact numbers will vary, this type of funnel exists in all sales campaigns. It is critical to develop a formula that works and to stick with it. Many entrepreneurs make the mistake of not continuing to fill the front end of the pipeline once they start processing opportunities.

Of course, it's a lot more fun to work active deals than to make cold calls and prospect. Nonetheless, entrepreneurs can't just hope opportunities will appear. They must go after them at all times. It's a numbers game that requires your ongoing participation.

In the beginning, TSI was a two-man operation. Both Mark and I did things that other workers took care of back when we worked for large corporations.

We found it helpful to build a workload schedule along with a duties roster. Here's how that schedule looked:

T. G.: Prospecting: 2 hours per day
    Marketing: 1 hour per day
    Vendor relation building with sales organization: 2 hours per day
    Financial activities: 2 hours per day

Process tracking: 1 hour per day
Misc.: 1 hour per day

M. O.: Prospecting: 2 hours per day
Technical review: 4 hours per day
Vendor relation building with tech staff: 2 hours per day
Misc.: 1 hour per day

This schedule gave us a roadmap for our daily operation. Although this plan would be interrupted, we stuck to it most of the time until we began to expand our staff after the first year.

We were well organized, but many things came up that we had not anticipated. Finally, we got our first order. It was for a $1,700 memory upgrade. I drove out to pick up the purchase order and brought it back along with a six-pack of beer. I didn't want to blow all of our profits, but a small celebration was in order.

The supplier we purchased the memory upgrade from made me put it on my credit card, because we did not have any terms established. I thought that was fair enough, but we needed terms fast. What if we had received a $50,000 order? Again, cash flow management is what makes or breaks most businesses. You must be prepared to float your accounts receivable while building both credit and revenue. This is where the rubber meets the road with all start-up companies. You must have cash to get off the ground. Credit cards will offer a quick but dangerous avenue to accomplish this. Paying 16 percent interest will kill your enterprise fast. This is what also separates the true entrepreneur from those who are "thinking, dreaming, but not rolling the bones."

Taking your life savings or borrowing against an asset like the equity in your house is very hard to do, both logically and emotionally. It is the single main reason most people never get to the starting line of realizing their dream.

Entrepreneurs must also be adaptable in the beginning. After being in business for two months, we got our first real big break. We received a $260,000 order for a twenty-workstation transaction. By then, we had a line of credit and were able to process and fulfill the order. The customer wanted us to install the equipment over the weekend so it would not disrupt their workflow. We agreed and coordinated the order with the shipping company.

Mark and I showed up bright and early on Saturday morning. I thought I would just oversee the installation and drink coffee. Although we usually wore suits, for this Saturday event I wore a pink shirt with a sweater tied around my neck and nice linen pants.

I had never been on-site for an installation. Mark laughed out loud when I appeared with coffee and doughnuts. He told me my task was to unbox all the monitors and desktops, and he would load all the software and network everything together. I walked into the shipping and receiving area and found more than fifty boxes on pallets. Mark gave me a box cutter and said, "We don't have all day, so get to work." But I was the president of the company! Well, he knew I couldn't install software and network twenty engineering workstations together. So I dug in, cutting, lifting, moving, and sweating. It took more than three hours for this task, and by the time I was finished I was covered in packing material and dirt from head to toe.

Years later, Mark still loves to tell this story about the President of TSI learning how an installation really goes. He tells everybody the only thing missing was I wasn't smoking a cigarette and wearing a tuxedo jacket. But I learned that you do what needs to be done to be successful, period.

Over the years, I have done almost everything in our office, including:

- Installed office furniture
- Set up our accounting system

- Invoiced, performed collection duties, and issued purchase orders
- Written contracts
- Done payroll
- Installed a phone system
- Managed numerous people
- Made coffee

Plus, I did an endless number of installations for clients, including running cables in every part of a building. And yes, returning to my roots, shoveled snow from driveways and parking lots.

The life of an entrepreneur is filled with an endless number of requirements, some anticipated and many not. To succeed, you must be willing and able to take on any and all tasks.

Technical Solutions Christmas Party, 2001

Technical Solutions Team Picture, 2002

31

History

The purpose of this book is to not only provide a history of my entrepreneurial quest, but more importantly, to also give you, the reader, advice and direction in your own quest. I have intentionally avoided spending a lot of time on TSI, but this chapter summarizes my experience with the company.

I started TSI in August 1992. Mark Oakes and I were the entire company in the beginning. The purpose of TSI was to sell complete turnkey computer systems to engineering companies in metro Detroit.

After being in business twelve months, I set off on a mission to add other products and people to TSI. I constantly asked our customers what products they considered best in class and were interested in purchasing. I wanted to start offering database products. My approach was each time to consider the following tactics:

1. Ask ten to fifteen IT managers what database they used and why. What did they like and dislike about the product?
2. Attend product trade shows and look at all the similar products being offered in the market.
3. Reach out to the channel managers presenting the products I was most interested in and then meet with them. Ask about the market, customers, plus potential.

This process usually took three to six months to complete. It cost a lot to launch a new product and I didn't want to rush to judgment and pick the wrong product for my company.

TSI grew every year in product offerings, employees, and revenue and profit. In eighteen years, we grew from revenue of $400,000 to $30 million. Our employee count went from 2 to 47. Along the way, more than 200 people worked for TSI. Our customer base grew to 125 regular accounts. We offered 84 different technologies representing more than 20 vendors.

Along the way, I decided my goal was to sell TSI instead of keeping the company for my children. Also, I was interested in wealth. Although I was making a lot in salary and bonuses, I knew that the real payday comes when you sell your company.

In 2003, I sold a portion of TSI to Detroit Technologies. However, I remained the president and still owned 49 percent of the company. The company continued to prosper and grow after that. We had great years in 2006 and 2007; our profits were in the millions. The best time to sell anything is when it's at its peak

I convinced the other owners to sell the company in April 2008 to a private equity firm, the Gores Group. I still ran the day-to-day operations, but now they made all of the decisions. This is typical with many private equity firms; they purchase companies and ask the existing management to stay on to run it. Their motivation is to invest, trim costs, grow the company, and then sell for a profit. The original goal on their part was to add or bolt on other similar companies to increase our revenue and profits.

Unfortunately, in the fall of 2008, the world economy melted down. General Motors and Chrysler declared bankruptcy and reorganized. This had a profound effect on our local economy in and around the Detroit metropolitan area. Many businesses closed and the unemployment skyrocketed. TSI cut back and remained profitable, but barely. The private equity firm had to borrow millions and inject the cash into TSI. Private equity firms have only one goal—to get a significant return on their investment—and if they can't do this, they get out.

After another three years, in October of 2010, they closed TSI. I, along with all our employees, were shocked. The day the announcement was made was a very disturbing and sad day. A lot of tears were shed. I set a new goal: to get all of the TSI employees a new job. This turned out to be easy because my key competitors wanted our well-educated and trained employees.

They also wanted access to our accounts. Within three days, most of my employees started new jobs. Although most longed for "the good old days" at TSI, they forged on in their new roles. Also, a major national computer company wanted to enter the Michigan market, so they hired some employees to gain a foothold. After thirty days, every one of my former employees had a new job, including Mark. The reason was simple: every single TSI employee was experienced, had a great reputation, and possessed all the necessary skills to contribute to a company's success.

I could not believe TSI had come to an end. However, I took great pride in the fact that all of the TSI employees were able to move on and provide for themselves and their families. Most start-up companies never last one year, let alone two or three. We had a great run for eighteen years. All companies eventually evolve and change or get eaten up along the way. In the end, I sold the company and lost the decision-making ability. I don't regret my decision to sell, because I clearly understood I was turning the decision-making power over to the Gores Group. While I would have liked to have been able to make all the major decisions for TSI, I felt that selling was the best move for me and my family. I also felt that the private equity firm would bring added management, insight, and capital to grow the company. That was their plan; however, the economic tsunami changed all of that. My goal was to sell the company at the right time and maximize my income from the transaction. After eighteen years and countless sixty-hour weeks, not to mention the investment I made to start the company, I felt I deserved it. I wanted financial security for me and my family, and I accomplished just that in the sale of TSI.

32

Moments

In 1998, my dad was getting sick all the time, cold after cold and occasionally some other bug. This was a man who was never sick a day in his life until then. We all insisted he see a doctor and, begrudgingly, he did.

After a number of tests, the doctor asked my dad to return to see him. Bad sign, I figured. The doctor told my dad he had chronic lymphoma, or leukemia. We were all shocked. I wondered why bad things had to happen to good people. This was just not fair.

My dad worked forty-five years, retiring just a few years before this diagnosis to enjoy the fruits of his labor. Now this? I was very mad at everyone, including God. My dad told me this news at lunch while eating a cheeseburger with fries and a beer. He said, "This is no big deal. A lot of people get much worse stuff, and besides, this is chronic leukemia, not acute. With acute, the progress is much faster." He said that some people never die from this form of leukemia and most live for years with it. Always the positive guy, my dad never, ever complained about all the challenges he faced.

As in most families facing a crisis, we all talked a lot among ourselves. My sister, Kathy, was devastated upon hearing the news. She had such love for and was so devoted to my dad. My brother, like me, thought it was an unfair deal. My mom, the nurse as always, felt modern medicine would help.

My solution: Let's go on a boys' trip to Florida. My mom did not like this idea at all, but in the end, she thought it would be good for all of us . . . little did she know. We decided on Fort Myers. Our great-aunt lived in the area, and we could see her as well as relax. However, we did not know Fort Myers was a huge spring break destination for college kids. My dad was diagnosed in February, so we decided to go for the week of St. Patrick's Day, another great idea. My dad was feeling just okay, but he was game. My brother was living in New York, but we all flew in to Fort Myers at about the same time. The airport was crawling with college kids. We had no idea they were all going to the same place as us.

It was when we pulled up to our hotel that it became very clear that the entire city was loaded with kids on spring break along with baseball fans going to any number of professional baseball spring training games in the area. The beaches were jam-packed with college kids having the time of their lives.

Both my brother and I had gone to Fort Lauderdale, Florida, for our spring breaks in college, but my dad had never witnessed anything like this scene. He took one look at this environment and his health improved 100 percent. My mom's last instructions were to take it slow and easy, no drinking or staying out late. Well, in this environment, that was never going to happen. We would hang at the beach all day, then have happy hour, then out to dinner and later head to the bars.

My brother Rob, our dad, and me.
Fort Myers Beach, Florida, 1998

We were the Three Musketeers. Every place we went, everyone else was young. In we would go and sit at the bar. Occasionally, someone would approach us and ask why we were there. Usually, my dad would jump in with a comment like, "Just like you, we are college students on spring break." Then he would go on, "I'm a Sigma Chi. What fraternity or sorority are you in?" Only my dad could get away with this. He was the hit every place we would go. As time went on, he would explain that we simply came to Florida to escape Michigan's cold weather and didn't know this was a big spring break destination. Some kids would talk with him and us for just a few minutes. Many would hang around and talk for a long while.

My dad loved talking with college kids, and most of them enjoyed conversing with him as well. He never mentioned the leukemia and never overstepped his boundaries. My dad would always ask them about college and what they hoped to do with their lives. And when asked, he would give his advice and insights. Kid after kid would tell my brother and me how cool our dad was. After a few nights in the same bars, we knew most everyone. My dad was like; "The Old Man of the Sea" sharing his wisdom with those who sought it.

Gotshall Men, 1987
My brother Rob, my son T.J., my dad, and me

We played golf, then rented a boat and went out on the ocean, and ran the streets of Fort Myers. It was the best time the three of us ever had together. Every night, we would sit up late and talk about every part of our lives. We reminisced about everything, including the camping trip we took years earlier. My dad said this was a much better time, 80 degrees, great beaches with college kids everywhere, wonderful meals, and late nights versus 40 degrees, sleeping on the cold ground in a sleeping bag, and eating half-cooked fish.

After we returned home, the planning for the next trip started right away. And, in fact, we returned to Fort Myers three more times over the next five years.

My dad was pretty sick during one of the trips, but he said we would go no matter what. And we did. Plus, we still did all the crazy stuff as before. We missed a few years because his pneumonia was so bad. In February 2004, we again planned a trip.

My dad was game to go once again, but this time my mom, sister, and brother didn't think it was such a great idea. However, I persisted. As before, I set up reservations for the same hotel, the Sea Watch by the Beach, along with plane reservations. Yet this trip was not meant to be made.

On March 5, my brother, Rob, who had moved back home from New York a few years earlier to be with our dad, called and told me dad was in the hospital in Ann Arbor, and I should go—now. I arrived to find my dad in intensive care, surrounded by machines and a lot of tubes attached to him.

He was breathing with the aid of a ventilator. I thought, *How strange being on the other side of this situation.* I recalled all those times when I was in the hospital as a kid struggling with asthma and breathing with the aid of a ventilator. Now my dad was the patient. The prognosis was not good at all. In fact, nobody thought my dad would see the next day. However, he did and after two days, he was transferred to a patient floor.

Yet he was still not doing very well. He had a feeding tube, and all kinds of antibiotics were being pumped into him, with no success. My sister, Kathy, came home from New York and we basically moved into the hospital. We took shifts at night, but for the most part all of us were always at his side.

Four days into the ordeal, Dad had a burst of energy. It was very strange. He sat up in bed, and we all had a great time talking about the past. However, with his three kids all home and in the room, he turned to me and said, "I know just what's going on. I understand why all of you are here now."

I replied, "Everything is going to be great. We are just figuring out who is taking you back home to Plymouth and when. Besides, it's time for you to start your spring lawn cleanup. Those leaves and branches aren't going to just jump into the bags themselves. Plus, we are set for the boys' return trip to Fort Myers."

He just stared into my eyes and smiled but said nothing. He knew his time had come. We filled his private room with pictures of family, grandchildren, and friends. We brought in a CD player and played his favorite music: Frank Sinatra, the Mills Brothers, and Dean Martin.

On the eighth morning, after being at the hospital from 1 a.m. to 9 a.m., I returned home. I had just fallen asleep when my wife, Marti, woke me up and told me to return to the hospital. I knew what had happened. I drove the forty-five minutes back to St. Joe's knowing this would be the last time I would see my father; I was filled with grief and disbelief. I quickly parked and ran into the hospital and down the hallway. Both my brother and sister were standing outside Dad's room.

On the door was a picture of a rose. I went in, and my mom was sitting on the corner of the bed. She looked up and said, "Your father is gone. Come and say good-bye." As I stood over my dad's lifeless body, I couldn't believe he was gone. I now understand why most people have to see their loved one in this state. Otherwise, you can't come to terms with the death of someone so important to you. Standing before my dad's hospital bed, I started to cry and touched his cheek. I couldn't utter one word or even a sound. It was like the blood and breath had been drained from my body. My mom said, "Everything will be okay." But I knew it was not true. She was trying to comfort me when the guiding light in my life was now no longer there to guide me. Marti and my children—I have more love for them than anything. My mother, sister, brother, along with all my brothers- and sisters-in-law—I also love them very much. However, my father was my mentor, hero, and best friend. Life without him would now have an irreplaceable, large hole in it. And it still does. The void is impossible to fill.

My dad and me after I purchased my first rental property, 1987

33

Last Lunch

The last lunch I had with my dad will stay with me my entire life. It took place three weeks before he was hospitalized.

We had lunch every Friday for twenty years. Our last lunch took place at Peabody's in Birmingham. The ironic thing is, it was in February and we almost canceled it because there was a huge snowstorm. I got to the booth first and brushed off the snow from my coat and hat. As my dad entered the restaurant, I could see that he was covered in snow as well and he looked ill and moved very slow. However, as he approached the booth he looked into my eyes and smiled broadly; he still had that twinkle in his eye. The very first thing he said was, "Maybe we both should have taken a snow day and not ventured out today." Yes, we again talked about my snow shoveling business and just how it started all those years ago.

We talked about how this journey might never have taken place if I wasn't interested or willing to venture out and shovel snow forty years ago. He said, "Maybe, but I would have continued to push you until you discovered the burning desire to become an entrepreneur. Because I knew deep down this was your true destiny."

My dad continued:

I never felt the right situation and opportunity
existed for me to make the leap into an entrepreneurial

quest. However, as your father, I just knew you would be great and successful at it.

You see, the life of an entrepreneur is a fascinating journey. You must be willing to take on any task or challenge, no matter how insignificant or grand.

Your attitude must at all time be up to any required challenge. The rewards can be endless. You will be called on to make decisions you are not currently aware of and deal with a wide assortment of situations. But that is the beauty of the quest.

Remember to keep your eye on the goal.

The most important thing is never lose your head. Deal with everything with as little emotion as possible. When you do encounter something unexpected, do the following:

- Take a moment to review all the facts.
- Think or write down all the possible solutions with the corresponding results.
- Look at all aspects of what your desired outcome should be.
- Make a final decision and move forward with it.
- Be open to modifying your path but only after careful analysis, and stay on course.

This was the last entrepreneurial advice my dad gave me. As I think back on it, I know he knew the end was near for him. He wanted to make one last point that would stick with me.

Have a plan and be determined. Maintain a positive attitude at all times. Finally, deal with all issues, both good and bad, with no emotion and move on. The journey will be grand.

My Dad's planner with every Friday noted with lunch with me.

Part III

Roadmap to Successful Entrepreneurship

In the first two sections of this book, I covered the evolution of my entrepreneurial quest. This third and final section gives you anecdotal building blocks that I feel will help you become a successful entrepreneur in today's economic climate.

34

A Natural Entrepreneur?

"Winning is not a sometimes thing, it's an all the time thing. You don't win once in a while. You don't do things right once in a while . . . you do them right all the time. Winning is a habit."
—Vince Lombardi (1913-1970),
Green Bay Packers coach

It has been said many times that there is no such thing as a natural athlete or a naturally brilliant person or . . . a natural entrepreneur.

All true. Our genetic mapping plays only a small role in our potential disposition. However, think about what is happening when we watch a skilled golfer make the final putt to win the U.S. Open or a wide receiver make a leaping catch in the end zone to win the Super Bowl. Or contemplate the billionaire you just read about whose company is making yet another purchase. Or recall a concert you attended where you watched and listened to your favorite musician perform a great show.

How is this possible? Did such success just happen overnight? Why not you?

Did this person get some major break in life?

The reason all of the individuals described above experienced success is simple: They had a goal, developed a plan, and worked an endless numbers of hours, days, and years to get to this point.

You, too, can be this highly successful person—if you are willing to make it happen. Becoming a great entrepreneur is not different from other types of success. It requires the same discipline, hard work, and preparation. My dad felt there were two main differences between all the above-mentioned winners and the rest of the masses: (1) continuous and unyielding commitment and (2) doing the right thing all the time.

Also, the entrepreneurial type of person is always analyzing and thinking about how to improve products or services, or inventing completely new products to improve the lives of everyone. If you observe any situation in commerce and say to yourself, "If I was running this place, I would offer the following additional products . . ." or, "I would better serve the customer by doing the following . . ." you may have the entrepreneurial spirit. The classic entrepreneur sees endless upside along with opportunity by improving and creating. And when you see and feel this, your heart rate will increase just imagining it.

If your thoughts coincide with this type of analysis, you are well on your way to becoming an entrepreneur.

35

Setting Goals

"The first and most important thing about goals is having one."

—Geoffery Albert (1079-1142),
French philosopher and priest

All of our lives we deal with goals. Sometimes they are goals of our own choosing, and sometimes the goal has been set for us by another person, such as a parent, teacher, or coach. Goals can be lofty and big, like becoming the captain of the football team or president of the company you work for. On the other hand, they can be simple and small, like working out three times a week or finishing a book you are reading. For the entrepreneur, goals are where it all starts. This may seem obvious and oversimplified; nonetheless, you should spend a lot of time and thought considering the goals you want to pursue. In a quiet, comfortable place, sit down with a notebook and write down your goals one after the other. Again, they can be both big picture and little picture. Here are some examples:

- I want to be self-employed.
- I want to run my own company.
- I want to be rich (almost everyone has this one) and independent.

- My company should be in the . . . commercial real-estate field, furniture business, computer field, interior design consulting area, construction field, or whatever.

Your goals need to be specific and well defined.

They should also be targeted: I want to buy and operate student rental properties in East Lansing to serve the students of MSU. A targeted goal aims at a defined market, e.g., MSU students living off campus.

The purpose of this exercise of goal setting is to get a start.

Don't stop and judge or edit the goals right now. This should be a free-flowing process. It is building block #1. After you're finished writing, set your notebook aside; review these goals in a few days and then again in a few weeks. Evaluate just how you feel about them and then modify your goals, if needed. Your next step will be to develop a plan with tactics on just how to reach your goals. If you have a trusted advisor, or just someone you respect, you may want to bounce these goals off of that person. Also, you should set a specific time line with dates for achieving each specific tactic and goal.

Your goals will lead to a mission statement, which will lead to your business plan. I spent six months translating my goals into the business plan for Technical Solutions. The Internet has many sites outlining how to develop your business plan; I would recommend checking out a few such sites.

36

Passion

"There is no substitute for passion in anything
you hope to be proficient at accomplishing."
—Thomas Gotshall,
entrepreneur and author

Passion is certainly part of the "secret sauce" to becoming a
great entrepreneur. Actually, it's the key to becoming really good
at anything in life. You will either possess passion for something,
or not. Although many things in life can be taught or learned, the
burning sensation from passion will simply exist in you or not. When
you see someone with passion for something, it is very obvious.

My three kids are pure examples of individuals with passion. All
three are great students; however, the contrast between sports and
school is profound.

My oldest daughter, Kristen, is passionate about tennis. In
high school, she wanted to practice all the time. She played USTA
(United States Tennis Association), took lessons from pros, and
dragged her younger sister, Erica, out to tennis courts all the time
so she would have someone to hit with. I remember reading the
newspaper one morning when I suddenly heard and felt rhythmic
banging throughout the house. Bang, bang, bang. The sound was
without interruption. The noise came from the garage area of our

house. I walked through the house toward the garage and entered it from the mudroom. The closer I got, the louder the noise got. Bang, bang, bang. When I opened the door leading to the garage, I saw Kristen smashing a tennis ball against the garage door. She was totally focused, and I startled her. "Hi Dad-e-o, I hope you don't mind me hitting a few volleys against your garage door," she said upon finally seeing me. I inspected the door and other than many round dirt marks, I couldn't see any damage.

I asked, "Why are you banging balls off my garage door instead of running up to the school and using the hitting wall?"

She replied, "Dad, it's Sunday and the fences are all locked. I didn't have enough time to drive to the courts across town, and I just felt the urge to work on a few things with my ground strokes."

She needed to "get her fix," as I like to call it.

My other daughter, Erica, has a passion for volleyball.

She asked me to buy a regulation volleyball net for our backyard, so she could work on her position and spiking the ball. She is an outside hitter. The goal in this position is to get set by someone in the back row and then slam the ball over the net for a "kill." The only problem with practicing this was that Erica needed someone to set her. Kristen also played volleyball, but she was off at college. That left Marti, my wife, T.J., the youngster, and me. We all learned how to do a proper set for Erica. Hour after hour, before practice and after practice and all weekend long, this would go on. She got really good at this position and earned a starting spot on the varsity team, which went on to become state champions.

One day Erica complained of soreness in her shoulder. However, a big match was coming up, so she would only let us ice her shoulder each night, and she would not go to a doctor. The day after the match, she couldn't move her right arm. We took her to an orthopedic specialist. He examined her and ordered an MRI. The results indicated three tears in her labrum. That is the area on your back just below the shoulder. The doctor told us that when this happens, people usually get one tear and can't lift their arms; two tears would be very painful; but three tears was unreal.

When the doctor asked Erica about this pain, she replied, "Yes, it did hurt a little, but we are in the late stages of the season, and it's all about getting to and winning 'States,' so like everyone, I needed to put up with a little pain." Even today when we reminisce about volleyball, Erica says she would probably practice to the degree she did, because she felt a burning need to improve and reach her full potential. And there was no substitute for all the practice.

My son, T.J., plays both football and lacrosse at his high school. He loves both sports. However, the lacrosse program has won seventeen of the past nineteen state championships. He currently is on junior varsity, but the prize is making varsity. T.J. asked if I would buy a hitting wall for him to practice on. After all, banging lacrosse balls against the garage door would make endless dents. Also, I wasn't very good at catching and passing with a lacrosse stick. By his freshman year, he had already played for four years, and I couldn't give him a good workout. I told him he had to research the "hitting wall" and tell me how much it would cost and how to get one. About thirty minutes later, he presented me with a printout with pricing and ordering instructions. The cost was $200 plus shipping, not to mention "some assembly required."

I, of course, told him that was a lot of money, but he did have a birthday coming and maybe . . . Anyway, I ordered the hitting wall and gave it to him for his big day. As expected, we had to put it together immediately. The next day was a school day. The routine was we got up around 6:45 a.m. to get things rolling. However, I awoke at 6:00 a.m. to the sound of a ball hitting a lacrosse hitting wall. Normally, getting T.J. up for school requires a lot of persistence. In other words, he is not a morning person, especially on a school day. I made my way downstairs and out our backdoor. Sure enough, I found T.J. standing in our backyard in a T-shirt and boxers with his lacrosse stick, throwing the ball repeatedly against the wall. I said, "T.J., what in the world are you doing?"

He replied, "Dad, isn't it obvious? I'm working the wall and practicing."

"Yeah, but it's 6:00 in the morning."

He continued, "I know. I have to have breakfast and get off to school, so that's why I'm out here now."

The thought never crossed his mind that this was strange that he was up earlier than he ever was and that he was standing in the backyard in boxers and a T-shirt banging a lacrosse ball against a practice wall.

When you are passionate about something—whether it's sports, music, another hobby, or a business interest—you don't have to force yourself to work at it. You will become obsessed with doing things you're passionate about. You would rather be engaged with it than doing almost anything else. It doesn't even feel like work; it simply consumes you, and you want to perfect whatever it is.

My three kids, like most kids, have to be told and often pushed to do their chores and fulfill other responsibilities. However, with their sports, I found they were so passionate that I had to sometimes tell them to stop practicing and do other things.

When you find a vocation you are truly passionate about, your potential for success skyrockets. Plus, you will truly enjoy just what you are doing. It doesn't become that four-letter word—*work*.

Rather, it becomes pure pleasure. You will know if you are truly passionate for something or not. I feel it's required to be successful as an entrepreneur, because it keeps you going when things get tough.

37

The Guide, Flashlight, and Map

In the summer of 2010, my daughter Kristen did a "study abroad." She went to Paris, Rome, and Florence. Being a college student is rough these days! Her professor and mother thought this was a necessary undertaking to round out her education. The professor was in charge of the programs . . . hmmm? Plus, she's an accounting major, which I felt wouldn't really be enhanced by the European experience. Nonetheless, Kristen and twenty other kids went off on their adventure.

The rest of the family joined her in Europe at the end of her semester there. We visited many wonderful places, including Notre Dame, the Louvre, the Eiffel Tower, Vatican City, St. Petersburg, and the Trevi Fountain.

We had hired a guide. I would recommend this, because they have a tremendous amount of knowledge; they know just where to go; plus, their certification allows them to go to the front of the lines. The line to get into Vatican City alone takes two or three hours to get through. But with the guide not only did we get to the head of the lines, we were allowed in forty-five minutes before the crowds. Standing in the Sistine Chapel with just our family and guide was alone worth the expense.

The Roman catacombs were thought-provoking for me. The catacombs are just outside of Rome, next to the Coliseum. When approaching the catacombs, our guide said the place even made her nervous. This is where the middle class was buried during the Dark Ages.

As we descended into the catacombs, our guide told us you could get lost "forever" down here. "When archaeologists first discovered the catacombs, many of them would just disappear; weeks, months, or years later, they would be found dead," she said. The tunnels spider every which way and each passage looked just like the last endless tunnel.

It dawned on me that this is what every entrepreneur faces at the beginning of his or her entrepreneurial journey. Ahead lies a tunnel, dark and surrounded by walls filled with bodies. Sounds great, huh? Well, it's not that bad. However, to navigate through the catacombs of Rome, you must have a guide, a flashlight, and a map, plus experience. It's the same for the entrepreneur starting out. You need your own guide, flashlight, and map.

So where do you find this guide?

My dad was my guide, but you might find guidance from a consultant or someone you know who has been there already and is willing to offer advice. You might rely on books you have read or even the Internet to find guidance. Still, it's best to have a sounding board to bounce thoughts and ideas off of.

The map is your business plan. It must detail every step you'll need to take on your journey just like a map helps you move from point A to point B.

The flashlight is your faith, along with someone who believes in you. At times we all need encouragement and someone who supports us no matter what crisis we face at the moment. This could be a spouse, a good friend, or your father or mother.

Just as when finding your way through the catacombs, all three of these parts are required for a safe and sustained entrepreneurial journey.

38

Your Beginning Tool Box

Once you have finally decided you are going to launch your entrepreneurial quest, you will need to have a "tool box." The investment in this tool box will be about $75. So now it's time to start investing. The following is you launching pad:

1. Business cards: Once you have named your company and designed your logo, go spend the $15 for 500 cards. You will begin to have business discussions with many different people about your new company. Before or after these discussions, people may want your card. This is not an old-fashion notion. It will validate your quest and leave behind a reminder for whomever you talked with. This may be a friend, a banker, a prospective investor, or maybe a future customer. Imagine you are at a Christmas party and after the small talk, someone is interested in hearing about your new idea and just maybe this person invests in start-up companies. After the conversation, he or she says, "Sounds like an interesting idea; how about a business card and I will call you in a few days to continue our discussion." You don't want to stumble around looking for a scrap of paper and pen and scribble down your phone number. This will probably end up in his or her pocket and lost, along with your appointment and opportunity. A business card will

add legitimacy and professionalism to you along with your idea. Also, don't be cute with a zany design or colors. The card should have a simple white background, black or blue printing that includes your complete legal name plus cell or land line number and your e-mail address. As for your title, you can put CEO/President or not have a title at all. Use standard business card sizing. When I get a card that is larger or smaller than the typical card, I'm annoyed because it won't fit into my stack or rolodex.

2. Elevator pitch. You must have a concise pitch about your idea or company. It should have an opening statement detailing your idea as well as your mission statement and a few benefits. You should practice and practice this pitch or speech, which should last about two or three minutes. The reason it's called an elevator pitch is because you should be able to give it in the time it takes you and someone to ride in an elevator. Cost: $0. However, not having a good one could cost you a lot in lost opportunity.

3. Printed company or idea brochure. This should be professionally done and printed on thick quality paper. It can be two or three pages and should detail formally your company or idea. This brochure should include your mission statement as well as just what you are offering or details about your idea. This is meant to give to interested parties. Cost: about $40.

4. Pure conviction. You must feel this in your bones. Whenever you are talking with anyone about your idea, you must look them in the eyes and believe with all your being that this is the greatest idea since the beginning of capitalism. Don't sound desperate or crazy—this scares most people. However, you must be enthusiastic, confident, and unstoppable. Cost: $0.

5. Portfolio. You need something to carry into meetings that contains your tool box stuff. You don't need to spend a bunch

on an alligator or even real leather folder. You can buy a fake leather one for $20. After you make your first million, go buy the alligator one.

This is just a starting point; however, the small investment will be well worth it. Creating such a toolbox will step up your game and will build your confidence that you can make your dream a reality.

39

Recognizing an Opportunity and Continuous Improvement

I know many people today would say "There is nothing new to invent; all the really great and innovative things have already been invented or started." This would be a classic valley person statement. Well how about Facebook? In 2003, Mark Zuckerberg was a student at Harvard when he came up with the idea of Facebook. He originally wanted to socially network with other Harvard students. After writing this relatively simple program, he decided that if students at Harvard were interested in the media, then students at other universities and schools would probably be interested in connecting as well. Then the obvious: many, many other individuals would want to connect as well. As for Mark, he is now the youngest billionaire ever. He took a simple concept, used the power of the Internet, and ran with an idea.

Another great example of an individual who took an idea to new heights is Mr. Bill Pulte, the founder of Pulte Homes. The retired founder offers a clear case of seeing and capitalizing on an opportunity. I was at the house of one of his daughters for a small get-together once when Mr. Pulte walked past me and said hello. I noticed he was carrying a few screwdrivers. Curious, I followed him to a back porch. He set the tools down and inspected the hinges on the screen door. I asked him what he was doing. He replied, "Just fixing the door." Pulte Homes is a wildly successful company. They build thousands of residential homes each year. Surely he could have had someone come over and repair this door. I asked him why he was doing the repair. He said, "Why pay someone to come all the way over to do a repair I can do myself?" Great point, I thought.

I asked him how and why he started Pulte Homes. He told me the following story.

The Pulte Homes Story

After WWII, Bill Pulte got a job working for a general contractor. One hot summer day, he was up on a roof shingling it. He said it must have been 110 degrees on top of that roof. The owner of the construction firm drove up in a Cadillac, jumped out with a tall glass of iced tea in his hand, and yelled up at the crew. "You guys had better move your asses or you will screw up my closing on this dump!" Then the owner got back in his air-conditioned Caddy and drove off in a cloud of dust. Most employees would have simply declared that the boss was a jerk and then have gotten back to work. Mr. Pulte told me he made two critical decisions at that moment:

First, he would never treat any employee with such disrespect.

Second, if this jerk could be a residential developer, he could surely be one as well.

Bill and his brother purchased a lot and during their free time, built, marketed, and sold their first house. Then they did another and another and another. The need for quality affordable homes was great. World War II had recently ended and all those soldiers were returning home to get married, start a family, and buy a starter house.

Pulte Homes was incorporated in 1950 and went public in 1969. Today, Pulte is the number one residential home builder in the United States.

A true entrepreneur is always obsessing and thinking about inventing or starting an enterprise. Keep your mind active and write down your ideas. Constantly look at the world and consider what needs improvement. It's important to stay with what you know. I started TSI because ComputerVision was changing the model of how it interacted with customers and I saw a niche that I could fill in the industry. Plus, I already had years of experience in the computer industry as well as years of having an active entrepreneurial mind. It was clear to me that starting TSI was a good move and would provide a nearly endless opportunity. I knew it would be a lot of work, but I felt failure was not an option.

Mr. Pulte didn't invent building homes. He recognized that a great need for new homes existed and he perfected a way to build them quickly and economically. He developed a team of professionals and mass-produced a great product at an affordable price. Not magic, just a very smart entrepreneur. Plus, he treated employees with respect so they wanted to be a part of his team.

Shortly after starting TSI, I started an exercise I called "brain trust time." At the end of each work week, when everyone at the company was beginning to decompress, I would go to my conference room for two hours and gather my thoughts and reflect about the week. I had a notebook where I would record thoughts and ideas. I would contemplate just what we could improve upon or change to make the company better. This was my designated creative time. Sometimes I would come up with great ideas; other times I wouldn't come up with anything. Occasionally, I would pull in Mark for these sessions or other TSI employees, to bounce ideas off of. The point is that all entrepreneurs should have a scheduled brain trust time to reflect on what they are currently doing as well as time to plan and innovate new things for the future.

40

Agility

One day at lunch, I sat down and my dad said, "Ssssshhhh, can you keep a secret?"

"Of course I can," I replied. "Why, what's up?"

He said, "Do you think anybody would answer that question any other way?"

"Is this a trick question?" I pressed.

He went on, "No, it's not a trick at all. I'm just trying to make a point for you. Everybody loves a secret or juicy gossip or, more important for the budding or established entrepreneur, the next idea. It is critical that you never tell anyone what your idea is, especially during the planning stage. Many great ideas belong to someone else first. This is true of songs, opportunities, and especially great, innovative entrepreneurial visions. Countless people have taken others' ideas and run with them and made their fortune. Telling someone your secret will not benefit you at all."

"People will take another person's idea and run with it and not think twice about the consequences. Our courts are full of cases dealing with individuals suing each other over stolen ideas. Even Facebook had a major legal battle that resulted with an enormous financial settlement. Eventually, you must reveal your idea. However, first, protect it any way you can. Use the legal system for this whenever possible, with patents or trademark registrations. Don't just blab it to anybody. No reason to tell a friend for justification. If you feel the idea is 'worth it,' run with it alone."

Even though I clearly remembered this discussion, I made the mistake anyway.

I belonged to a private golf club and I knew the Ryder Cup, along with the PGA of America Championship, was coming to our club. I was a new member and I was playing golf with a friend, someone I thought I could trust. We had played many rounds together and shared a lot about ourselves during our time on the course. We talked about business and our personal lives.

When a residential home came up for sale across the street from the club entrance, I noticed right away. The professional golfers traveling to Michigan playing in these tournaments would potentially be interested in renting this house because of its proximity to the club, making it an ideal rental for them and their family members. Also, many corporations would rent houses for entertainment. They would put up large tents and invite customers for food and drinks before or after the day's activities at the tournaments. *So,* I thought, *why not purchase this house for all these upcoming tournaments?*

As we were walking down the first fairway, I said, "Hey I have a great but crazy idea. Why don't we buy that house across from the club and rent it out for all the tournaments coming to our club? I'm thinking we could go 50/50 on purchasing it, then rent it out for the upcoming events. We could advertise in *Golf Digest.* My company could launch a website for it as well. We could take digital pictures and post them on the site. If someone wanted more info, they could submit a request for a package of information and even schedule a tour. Also, we could probably list the property with a local real-estate firm that may be brokering houses for the Ryder Cup or PGA . . . ." I went on and on and on.

We talked about it for most of the round. As we concluded, I said, "Think it over and let me know what you think."

I made a number of mistakes. One was sharing the idea in the first place. The second was going on and on with all of my ideas. Also, I waited for him to respond without taking any action.

I remember telling my dad of the discussion. His question was, "If you think it's such a great idea, why don't you move on it yourself?" I thought it would be a fun project to do with my friend; we could work on it together. My dad's advice: "Partnerships seldom work in the long run. You managed all those rentals in East Lansing; why not this one as well?"

Two weeks after our discussion, I was driving into the club when I saw a sold sign in front of the house. *Damn, I blew it, I thought. Too slow to move on it, which was my fault.*

Later that day at the club pool, my wife, Marti, and the other women were all sitting around watching their kids. My friend's wife proclaimed: "We just made a great investment! We purchased the house across the street from the club. Our plan is to rent it out for all the tournaments coming to the club." Marti was speechless. She knew about my idea and the discussion I had earlier with my friend. She said nothing at the time, as all the women were praising the couple for their great idea. Later that day when we got together, she said, "You'd better sit down for this piece of news." She told me about the purchase and the couple's great idea!

I, too, was speechless, not to mention pissed. When I next encountered this friend, I told him he stole my idea. He responded, "Other guys were talking about the idea as well, and I felt I had to move quickly. You didn't invent the idea of buying and renting houses to pro golfers." My friend said he wanted to do it alone. I was in disbelief. How could I have been so stupid?

He moved quickly and left me and my idea in the dust.

Who do I blame for this happening? Not my golf friend, only myself.

Keep your ideas and entrepreneurial thoughts to yourself. Learn from my mistake. At some point, you will need to trust someone with your idea; just make sure you are careful and protect your entrepreneurial intentions.

41

Hiring

"You can dream, create, design and build the most wonderful idea in the world, but it requires people to make the dream a reality."
—Walt Disney (1901-1966)

Hire the best employees you can afford. The process requires a lot of planning and focus. Before you conduct one interview, write down exactly what you are looking for. This is my outline for a marketing director I was in need of.

> Job description: The position of Marketing Director will include lead generation for the sales department. The activities will include designing, managing, and conducting seminars. He/she will also do direct mailing campaigns each month. Also the quarterly newsletter will be the responsibility of the individual along with updating and managing the company website.
> Goals: Generate 50 new qualified prospects each year. Insure OEMs offset our marketing activities with funding.

Qualifications: Four-year college degree in marketing or similar area of study. Three to five years experience in computer or related field, along with positive references.

Keep everyone in the same time frame and control the process. First, get resumés from a headhunter, want ads, and the Internet. When I needed a Marketing Director at TSI, I created an ad and posted it on the Internet, both on our company website and on a job board.

I received 220 resumés. After my cutoff date, I compared the resumés with my job outline, which included the job description and qualifications. My goal was to pare down the 220 resumés to 8 to 12. My required qualifications included a college degree and marketing experience of three to five years. Ideal candidates would have computer or IT (information technology) experience. In a resumé, you can quickly pick this out. You don't have time to read them word for word, so just looks for key points.

In two hours I could get through more than 200 resumés.

Next, go back and read the 8 to 12 you've selected and then narrow it down to 6 to 8 great picks.

Designate one morning from 7 a.m. to 12 p.m. to conduct the interviews. Have a secretary call or email the candidates you want to meet.

Here is an example of what could be communicated:

Our firm, TSI, has received your resumé. We are conducting initial thirty-minute interviews and would like you to come in. The position of Marketing Director will include the following duties: Lead generation for the sales department, managing all of our customer events and writing our newsletter, and controlling the content of our website.

The compensation package includes a salary of $70,000-$80,000/year depending on experience, plus benefits and bonus. Please respond, so we may schedule an interview time.

This is a great screening tool, because you don't want somebody who is under- or over-qualified. Somebody might have an MBA from Harvard and expect to make $175K/year. Don't waste your time. Time is money. You don't have time to interview a dead-end prospect. This will also show prospective employees your professional process.

At the interview, get to the resumé and experience fast. Also check the candidates out in person. This is the best they will look. My dad said you can judge a person by their shoes. It's not that everybody can afford Allan Edmond shoes for $450. However, the condition, polished or not polished, laces tied or not (no kidding) is telling. Over eighteen years, I interviewed hundreds of people, and you would be shocked at the condition and style of their shoes. I was interviewing a candidate for a sales executive position, and a guy came in with a blazer, no tie, and tennis shoes. That interview lasted five minutes.

Fashion has changed over the years. However, people who did their homework before the interview and went to our website would learn a lot about us and be able to decipher our dress code so they could dress accordingly. In all of our pictures, every TSI male employee was in a suit and tie or blazer and tie; women were also in suits or blazers and skirts. The only exception would be pictures from our annual customer golf event in which we wore golf attire.

Also note if they arrive early and are prepared. I was always impressed with candidates who did their homework and reviewed our website.

After the first round of interviews, I would chop the list down to three candidates and invite them back for a one-hour interview and a meeting with the potential supervisor.

In these meeting we would cover the following with open-probe questions:

- Their experience (spend the most time on this)
- Their expectations or goals
- Why they want to work for the company
- How they can contribute to the company

Talk about the culture and your expectations. Read and observe them through this entire process. Say, "Tell me about yourself." This is a great way to learn about the candidate. Ask if they have questions. Remember, they should do 70 percent of the talking and you, 30 percent.

By law, you can't ask about certain things: their age, marital status, sexual orientation, or medical history.

By now, you should have an attorney. Ask for a written description of human resource laws, specifically around interviewing and hiring.

Most of this stuff you can figure out yourself. The year they graduated from high school and college will allow you to pinpoint their age. Ring=married, no ring=single . . . sometimes. For the most part, this stuff doesn't matter, but it will help you "frame" the person.

A great hire is priceless. A bad hire is an incredible time-sucking pain in the butt, often ending in termination and starting the process all over again, wasting time and money.

Also, do a background check, and check two references. Look up the candidates on Facebook and LinkedIn. This will reveal much information.

Have them fill out an employment application. Make sure it notes that they are an "at will" employee, which means you can terminate them anytime for whatever reason.

42

Employee Retention

"People that work together will win."
—Vince Lombard,
Green Bay Packers coach

Once you have good employees, keep them. This requires training them, compensating them fairly, and letting them know you appreciate their good work.

I had an open-door policy with my employees. I told them many times that if they had an issue with someone or something to come and see me. I was very approachable.

This alone is not enough. Survey your employees at the end of each year. People want to be positively recognized and be well compensated.

Also, they want to contribute to the "good of the order" of the company. In other words, they want to make the company successful. Really! This makes people feel better about themselves and their place of employment.

Before I started TSI, I worked for many bosses and organizations. Some were great, and some were terrible and didn't have a clue. I pledged I would always be fair but firm and very clear.

We selected salesperson of the month and year, with a plaque and $50 to $100. We did the same with sales support technologists.

You may think this is corny, but sending an employee home with a plaque and $50 works wonders. I felt good giving out these awards, and the people receiving them felt even better.

You must build a team. Our firm had a Monday morning meeting. Everyone, including employees in sales, sales support, administration, technology, and management, were required to attend.

I played music starting fifteen minutes before the meeting. The main purpose was to get everybody going on Monday after the weekend. The meeting would last thirty minutes.

At the weekly meeting, we would cover general company announcements and announce any new vendor relationship. We would also highlight a new customer or good sale from the week before, detailing how each group contributed: sales, administration, and technology.

Once in a while, I might give a sales support person or technologist $50 for "making a difference." I referred to it as "mad money" to be used for something crazy, not groceries or bills. Putting $50 in an employee's hand alone wouldn't convince them that your company is the greatest place to work. However, sometimes it's the little signs of appreciation that help in a big way. I also treated everyone with respect and dignity. Most important, I was consistent with my rules and judgment. No one was above the rules and we didn't have a boss's pet employee.

I also had a budget for continuous training and education. We sent employees to many classes and seminars, no matter where they were held. Most employees greatly appreciate the opportunity to enhance and increase their knowledge. We also had a university reimbursement program to assist employees who wanted to complete their formal education. A well-trained and educated staff will always make your organization better and ripe with new ideas. Our reputation locally was that our staff was very knowledgeable and well trained, and this paid off with new and loyal customers.

43

Awards and Accolades

Successful entrepreneurs have qualities such as knowledge, persistence, and creativity, just to name a few. One sure thing every entrepreneur should know is that it's the people you surround yourself with that will make the difference on whether your dreams and plans come together.

When I was a sales executive, I always wanted to be number one in the office, then the district, then the country, and finally, the entire world.

As a "freshman" sales representative starting off, I could only observe as different types of awards were handed out at the annual kick-off. All employees, but especially sales executives, are motivated by money and recognition. The one consistent thing I saw was that each award winner basked in the "sunshine"; plus it was all about "them." The team that supported the winner was lost in the shuffle. The technical support and administration personnel were left out.

I remember encountering one egomaniac winner after the awards banquet, in the hotel bar. He was holding court with his trophy proudly displayed, explaining to anyone who would listen how he "single-handedly" landed the biggest account the company had ever had. The transaction was for more than $10 million and growing. The great thing about the computer industry is once you land the big fish and get a technology "footprint," it will grow and grow as technology advances. Anyway, on and on he went. About twenty feet away, the technical staff that was critical to successfully landing this account sat mocking this guy. I heard one say, "This dope doesn't know how to spell the word computer, let alone assemble everything that encompasses the solution we sold to the customer." It's the way the system works, but this knucklehead forgot a key part of his team and just how the deal did get done. He wouldn't have had to do much to recognize his team; it's the little things that stick with people. I thought he should have talked about the team win. Humility is a virtue, and all he needed to do was to go over to that table and thank everyone involved in the sales campaign.

Be sincere, buy a round of drinks, and explain the truth: "I could never have accomplished this without each one of you." Or, "I'm proud to be your teammate and I'm looking forward to going back and getting another big fish with all of you." Simple, smart, and the truth.

I never forgot that smug SOB.

During my years of working for computer companies, I had my share of awards, and I always remembered this experience. I always made a point of taking care of the team first.

If I gave a speech, I recognized each team member at the beginning.

The company I started, Technical Solutions, earned and won a number of awards.

- Sun Microsystems reseller of the year
- INC 500 Fastest Growing Company in North America
- 2000-2010 Future 50 Fastest Growing Company in Metro Detroit. Ten years in a row, which was more than any other company in Michigan

I was awarded Entrepreneur's Finest of the Year in Technology, by KPMG (Klynveld, Peat, Marwick and Goerdeler) and The Detroit Chamber of Commerce, plus many other awards. But each time the company won, I only talked about the organization as one unit winning. We always would have a big party and involve spouses.

The best part for me was giving out Doe-Ray-Me (cash), not a crazy amount. But there is just something about cash. My normal practice was to hand the employee's spouse the cash and explain: "Your husband/wife puts in endless hours for our company. I know this is disruptive to a family. I appreciate your understanding. So this $250 is just for you to go blow on something crazy. You can't go buy groceries or gas or pay bills. The next time I see you, I hope you will tell me about your purchase. Enjoy and thank you for your support." Maybe it was trite, but it helped build a feeling of family in my company.

My dad was right, "Cash is king."

44

Team Building

"The main ingredient in stardom is the rest of
the team."

—John Wooden (1910-2010)
UCLA basketball coach
who won 10 national college championships

Be humble and check your ego at the door. For some
entrepreneurs this is hard.

All really successful entrepreneurs have big egos, from Bill
Gates to Donald Trump to Warren Buffet. Sometimes, ego alone will
drive us to keep on going. Yet you can't launch and build a company
by yourself; you need others. Many times, you must give the credit
to others. Remember recognition. You are the coach. You want your
employees (players) to develop and feel good about their success. As
they go, so goes the company.

The more you give to your team, the more you will get
from them.

You want a loyal and driven production team.

Building a sense of team is critical. At TSI, we had a variety of
employees—different religious beliefs, different cultures, different

social economic classes. Also, the personalities at the company ranged all over the map.

With such a makeup, of course we had our differences. With close to fifty employees, not everybody is going to love one another. What I was after was cohesiveness and positive results.

Communication is key and must flow with ease. At TSI, some of the best practices came from the employees themselves. Be open to their new ideas. Respect for one another only grows when employees really know their fellow employees. They should know what their background is along with their motivations in life and work and just what makes them tick.

Once a year we would have a team-building event, like a bowling tournament. Based on ability, I would divide the employees into teams. Everybody looked forward to this annual event. It created positive competition along with banter. On those days, we would have a morning meeting to discuss the state of the company. I would cover goals and just how we were currently stacking up, good things that were going on as well as things we needed to improve on. After that, we would caravan over to the bowling alley and spend the balance of the day bowling and hanging out together.

I felt that building a cohesive team would not be possible if employees did not really know one another. Although this occurred naturally with time, the team-building events helped forge those relationships. Our Monday morning meeting became an avenue to learn who we were working with as well. After an employee had been on board for a few weeks, they were required to present their life's history to the company at one of our Monday morning meetings.

It didn't matter what department they were in, most people, except sales executives, hated public speaking. Some would try to get out of the new employee presentations, saying: "I can't. Please don't make me do it!"

I was consistent and responded: "Everybody before you has done it. We all want to know more about you!"

They could use pictures, videos, music, or just their own words. I had a template and told them it should only last ten to fifteen minutes.

Employees would show pictures of themselves as kids in Little League or other sports uniforms or participating in some other organization or event. They'd talk about where they grew up and say something about their family. I will never forget Lan's presentation. She was from China and struggled somewhat speaking English.

She was an Oracle DBA (Oracle programmer) and was really, really good at her job but was shy beyond comparison. I asked one of the other women in the office to "tutor" her. Helen came to me and said, "Lan's got it, no help needed."

I was even nervous for her. At the beginning of the new employee presentations, I sometimes had to encourage people or break the ice due to their nervousness. Sometimes I would have to move it along or get out the hook and cut them off. But not with Lan.

She served green tea to everyone and played ancient Chinese music on the office CD player. Using a projector, she showed pictures of her home in China, a small house, really small, and people everywhere. "This is my mother, father, uncles, aunts, brothers, sisters, and cousins," she said

One of the sales executives asked, "Did they all live in your town or village or nearby?"

Lan said, "No, we all lived in the same house!"

Lan talked about her culture, background, and family. She was one of the hardest working employees TSI ever had. After hearing her story, I understood why, and so did everybody else at the company. Opportunity here, in the United States, is limitless. In China, if your grandfather was a ditch digger and your father was a ditch digger, you were going to be a ditch digger too. As for entrepreneurs, this is even truer. Yes there are many barriers of entry to the world of becoming an entrepreneur; nonetheless the opportunity does exist.

New employee presentations were an exercise that helped solidify us as a team. I know many people are uncomfortable speaking to a group of their peers; however, after they presented their story, every one told me they appreciated the opportunity to tell all of us about themselves. Also, everyone listening gained both an admiration for new members of our team and respect for who they were.

45

More Sales and Marketing

Marketing

Marketing is the juice, the activity that will drive your company's sales. Marketing and sales go hand in hand. The goal is to create a marketing campaign that will provide sales opportunities. In the bible of marketing, the 4 Ps are often discussed. They are the basic principles that all marketing events must have:

1. Product: A product or service that is featured
2. Price: A specific asking price for this product/service that is clear
3. Place: How, when, and where the product is obtained
4. Promotion: Details about the event that will drive the sales

In addition, I feel there is one more thing required: a call to action that the prospect must respond to. Without a required action for the prospect to perform in a specific time frame to get "in" on the opportunity, the sales potential will diminish. Automobile dealers conduct these types of events all the time.

For example, a Lincoln dealership will run a special on an MKS. It can be leased with nothing down and a payment of $350 a month for thirty-six months. But you must act quickly because the offer is only good until President's Day at North Brothers Lincoln in Troy.

The 4 Ps are clearly all covered in this offer: Product, Price, Place, and Promotion.

There are many books on marketing, plus the Internet has an endless array of information. You don't have to be a marketing genius to market your product or service. But some studying in this area will be very helpful.

Sales

Some entrepreneurs love and are great at this part of the puzzle. Some . . . are not. You must execute this aspect of owning a company to move your idea. Sales do not just happen. In the beginning of TSI, I was both the marketing director and sales executive. This was my experience and vocation. If you are not good—no, not great at this—get someone on board who can perform this function. The Internet could be helpful in introducing your product or service to the world. However, you still need someone to complete the deals and bring in the sales.

Here are a few basic tips:

- Define your territory. Who do you feel could use your offering?
- Understand all the customer's needs.
- Differentiate yourself and the offering.
- Sell benefits, not features.
- Make doing business with you easy.
- Get confirmation that you have understood the customer's problems and that you have solved those problems.
- Ask for the sale, and *shut up.*

The most important resource a sales executive has is his or her time. Do not ever waste it on an unqualified prospect. Sometimes it's hard to do. Some feel an "upfront" contract is the way around this. Simply stated: Get an agreement of sorts with the prospect. If you spend all your time understanding his or her needs and then provide the best solution at a fair price, this customer will give you the order. Somewhat tricky but if this applies to your offering and you can execute this methodology, all the better.

When I started my campus rental painting business, I fulfilled all of these basic pieces:

- My starting territory was Mr. Williams's rentals properties.
- His need was to get all thirty-two rentals painted for a low price.
- I differentiated myself by offering to complete all the required work that summer.
- The benefit was I would put the crew together and provide all the necessary equipment: truck and ladders.
- I made doing business with me easy; I had a solid plan to scrape and paint, and would get paid only after the completion of two houses.
- In our meeting, I asked for his confirmation that I completely understood all his painting needs. I asked if I was missing anything.
- I asked for the contract to paint all his properties, and I shut up and waited for his response.

There is nothing complicated about this. Yet, experience is a must. Every single sales person has to start with his or her first sales opportunity. I told every employee at TSI that he or she was a sales ambassador. "Selling can be very rewarding. You just have to stick with it and be persistent."

Fred Hill from John Smith's Clothing, from the previous section, was a natural at selling because he didn't appear to be selling. He understood his customers' wants, needs, and interests along with most of what they currently had hanging in their closets. He knew how to target them and provide new product. To be successful as an entrepreneur, you must know your target audience well along with their needs. You can shape your offerings based on this critical information.

46

Contracts

A Man's Word Isn't What It Used to Be

My dad always told me the following: "Say what you will do and do what you say." However, not everyone subscribes to this adage. He would also tell me that when you are an entrepreneur, you will deal with many types of people, and some are honest and some are not. Trust is a healthy feeling you should have toward everyone. Nonetheless, sometimes people will tell you something they will do and in the end, one of the following will take place.

They will have:

- Every intention of doing what they told you and do it.
- No intention of doing what they told you.
- Every intention of doing what they told you but will not fulfill their obligation for any number of reasons.

If you are going to make a business decision based on what someone tells you, always get it in writing, with a signature. Period. An e-mail will not hold up in court.

If someone is willing to commit to something, he or she should be willing to put it in writing. Even if you have to draft the agreement, just do it.

Make sure you get the following:

- The agreement must be on their company letterhead stationery.
- A date must be on the document.
- No weasel words should be in the agreement, allowing it to be voided if certain things happen or take place.
- A signature by a company officer.

If a salesperson agrees to something and puts it in writing, it means absolutely zero—because salespeople don't have the right to legally commit the company they work for to do or provide anything.

I recently had a president of a company agree to lease some space in a building I own. I had his word that he was going to complete the deal. I provided a lease, and he asked to have his chief administration office review it. Well, this turned into a month-long process, but he continued to promise me this was a "done deal." He even shook my hand on it. Finally, the lease was ready for signature. I received an e-mail from the administration office that it was a deal and I would receive the document in one day. You guessed it—he backed out.

My attorney told me I could file a lawsuit and take him to court. Anybody can sue anytime, anyplace, and for any reason these days. However, in the end I probably wouldn't win. Maybe I would have gotten some settlement but it was a long shot. Until you have it in writing, you don't have much. So get everything important to you in writing and signed.

Negotiating Contracts

You will also deal with endless contracts. When presented with a contract, you have two options: Read it and sign it, or have your attorney read it, make comments, and then either sign it or see to it that the attorney's recommended changes are made. By the way, every single attorney will find something he or she doesn't like in any contract.

Contracts can be very tricky. And, as I have advised, do what you know and get professional assistance in unknown areas. Because our company dealt with major OEMs like HP and Oracle, I knew they would never change their boilerplate agreements. We could spend thousands and thousands of dollars in attorney fees, request changes, and their response would always be the same: You can sign our Reseller Agreement and sell our products. Or you can disagree with our standard contracts and simply not be a reseller, period.

You have to make a value judgment in these situations. Use your resources (cash) for meaningful things. If you agree with the basic provisions of the contract and feel it is fair, go ahead and sign it.

However, for certain agreements, you must have legal representation. When I sold TSI, I hired the best M and A (mergers and acquisitions) law firm I could find. The buyer's attorneys and my attorneys took three months to finalize the contract. By the way, the process of selling my company from letter of intent to working agreement to final legal contract took a total of six months. And I was told this was fast! For actions like selling your company, I feel it's critical to get the best legal advice. Don Kunz with Honigman, Miller, Schwartz and Cohn is the best M and A attorney in the land, and he saved me countless times in my agreement with the Gores Group.

So, be patient with the most important contracts. The bottom line is you should have an attorney who is on your side. You should have open discussions on all legal matters, and your attorney should tell you when to use his or her services and when not to.

That said, in the end, the final decision on how to best use your resources must be yours.

47

Budgeting and Forming Your Company

Every year, I set up a projected family budget as well as a projected company budget. You should know just what your number is for both of these. In this book, we will focus on your company budget, though this is a great exercise for your household as well.

Begin by preparing a list of expenses on a monthly and annual basis. This list should include but not be limited to the following:

1. Payroll
2. Health care
3. Rent
4. Insurance
5. Supplies
6. Materials
7. Inventory
8. Equipment
9. Travel and entertainment
10. Interest and principal payments
11. Professional fees
12. Miscellaneous

Next forecast your revenue, with cost and gross margin, also on a monthly and annual basis. This forecast will give you a profit and loss projection, along with a cash-flow requirement. This process has been oversimplified to help you build your model. There are many books that will help in this area. Plus, check out the Internet.

Your CPA can be very helpful in this area. And yes, you should have retained a CPA before starting your company. This professional should also give you advice on the formation of your company, especially whether you should form an LLC or a C Corporation or a Sub-S Corporation. There are important tax and legal ramifications with this key decision. Make sure you consult a qualified CPA along with an attorney. However, the following are a few important definitions.

- A LLC, or Limited Liability Corporation, shares with a Corporation the limited liability attributes. Also, it shares with a partnership the ability of pass through income taxation at the owner's tax bracket. It is more flexible than a corporation and it is well suited for companies with a single owner.
- C Corporation is a corporation that under the United States income law is taxed separately from its owners. The initial tax may be at a lower rate; however, when you distribute net profits as bonuses, the money will be taxed at your tax bracket level—in other words, double taxation.
- Sub S Corporation is a corporation of between 1 and 100 shareholders and the net income or losses are passed through directly to the owners at their prevailing tax bracket.
- Inc. When you see this designation after a company name, it does not define the treatment of taxation. It is simply the formation of a new company under the laws of the state in which it is formed.

You don't need to be a CPA to form a company; however, consult with one before you designate this. All this information is on the Internet and, in fact, you can form your company online now.

48

Money

How you manage the profits and cash flow of your company will determine its longevity. There is a fine line between being frugal and being cheap. When it comes to spending money, people fall into certain camps: savers, spenders, or borrowers. Some have to spend to feel good about themselves.

Many billionaires are billionaires because of how they managed their money, especially in the start-up period and first few years. Sam Walton comes to mind. His story is a classic.

Sam started Wal-Mart in 1962 and was well on his way to success by 1974. Wal-Mart was growing and doing very well, and Sam was rich beyond his dreams. That year, Sam was in need of a desk. He found a damaged sheet of plywood, propped it up on two sawhorses, and used it as his office desk in his corporate headquarters. After a number of years, his secretary finally convinced him to replace it with a real desk. Years later, while being interviewed by the *Wall Street Journal*, Sam was asked about this. His reply was, "The sheet of plywood couldn't be sold and it made a perfectly good desk. I hate to waste anything, period. Just how do you think I grew this company and kept it going in the early years? I preserved cash while protecting the very existence of the company." Sam Walton became a billionaire and made all his children billionaires as well. Today, Wal-Mart employs 2.1 million people and has over 9,600 stores in 28 countries, according to their most recent fact sheet on the web.

This story may be a little extreme, but Sam was not comfortable blowing money. He drove a pickup truck and wore off-the-rack suits.

Saving and Planning for the Future

I believe everyone should have twelve months of cash saved to cover all expenses. My dad said this takes time. However, discipline is critical. If you lose your job, you must have "coverage." The ultimate goal is to have enough in retirement savings to cover all your living expenses through eighty-five or ninety years of age.

Along the way, don't ever live check to check. Save from day one. I know that in the beginning of your professional working career that is impossible. But after working three to five years, you should have a cushion.

Set a goal. After working one year, have X saved; after year two, have X+Y; after year three, have X+Y+Z. Keep this going and don't cut into this nest egg. If you need something new, start saving and don't just run out and put the purchase on a credit card, paying 18 percent interest! My dad told me I should have a zero dollar balance on all credit cards every month. Period.

Once you are rolling along in your career or your business is taking off, it's very tempting to "live high on the hog." After all you deserve it, right? Cars, trips, expensive clothes, and so on. Yes, you should reward yourself but set a goal and stick to it.

With employees and important customers, do what is expected from a financial standpoint. Is it necessary to take a big client out to an expensive restaurant and buy fine wine? Do the math. I based such decisions on the potential and existing return. If it makes "business sense," do it. At TSI, we purchased tickets to just about every event in the Detroit area: Red Wings, Tigers, Lions, and Pistons games. And then we used those tickets to entertain clients and reward employees.

Business entertainment is expected and generally you must make a value decision on the expenditure with results in mind. Events like going to dinner or attending sporting events with customers or vendors will turn the pure business relationship into a less formal, friendlier relationship and this is a positive outcome. You want to be viewed as a consultant, who is helping to solve a business need, not just a salesperson trying to slam dunk another deal for the sake of making a commission. As your relations grows from a formal relationship to a more relaxed one, your clients will trust you and your recommendations even more. It will greatly increase your business potential because people like to do business with people they know and trust.

However, you must budget for this expense and make sure your year is tracking. If business slows or you need to make spending cuts, cut entertainment.

I knew another computer company president whose firm was similar to TSI in many ways. I remember going to a Detroit Red Wings game and seeing his company name and logo painted in large bold print along the boards in the hockey arena. The next time I saw him at a vendor event, I asked him about those boards. He said it cost $35,000, but he also got four season tickets out of the deal, with a value of $1,200. I responded, "So the real value is $1,200 in tickets and $33,800 to stroke your ego."

I debated the cost, plus the need for this expenditure with him. I said, "Both of our target audiences are very specific. We are not trying to reach the general public attending a hockey game. Our audience is chief technology officers and technology personnel." He agreed with me, but his concluding remark was, "I feel it's cool to see my company name at the games and even occasionally on TV."

The computer business was growing like crazy at this time. All of us were making money and growing. The following year, however, things slowed just a little. This man's company went out of business, and he had to let everyone go. He hadn't planned on even a slight downturn in revenue and profits.

Sometimes I took frugality to extremes. Mark occasionally joked, "Ebenezer, please, please put another lump of coal on the fire."

The economy is very dynamic, with highs and lows. It has proven to be cyclical over time. The prize is staying in business for the long haul. At TSI, when things slowed a little, we had money in the bank, cash flow to keep going, and all of our employees had jobs. I would tell Mark, "I have to make sure we always have enough coal to make it through the entire cold winter or whatever downturn comes our way."

49

Leadership

Leadership means many different things. As an entrepreneur, you by default are the leader of your organization. As the leader, you set the pace and tone of your company. This does not mean you must give rousing speeches each day. Although it is a benefit if you are decent at firing up the troops and can give speeches. However what is more important is that you are the individual your team believes in. Your ideas and actions will define you as the leader. You must inspire and be confident in what you do. Your work ethic is critical.

I have had bosses who "goofed off" and then would yell at anyone who was not performing up to standards. I never respected this type of leader. Bosses who go off to play golf or take three-hour lunches and then return to work just to yell and criticize are bad managers.

As CEO or president, you should work harder than all of your employees. At TSI, I felt strongly about punctuality. We started at 8:30 a.m. sharp. That meant working, not standing around talking about some sporting event or TV show. My dad felt if you weren't fifteen minutes early, you were late. Period. I told all my employees this over and over.

I made it clear that general conversation was great. Get to work fifteen to thirty minutes early, get your coffee, socialize, etc., and then get going. It was the same for the end of the day; we finished at 5:30 p.m., not 5:15.

I learned this punctuality in sports. If practice was to start at 5:30 in the afternoon, it started at 5:30 sharp. You did not even think about showing up after 5:15. If you let one person slip and slide, everybody else will do the same thing. At TSI, I was fair but firm and consistent. If Joe could be late, why not everybody? Ten minutes became twenty minutes and so on.

Our customers deserved the very best from us. They knew TSI was open for business at 8:30 a.m. sharp. I had our receptionist come in at 8:00 just in case someone called before 8:30.

Over-serve and be professional.

I am also a big believer in MBWA: Management By Walking Around. Every day was busy at TSI and filled with meetings. Yet almost every day, I made it a point to walk the entire building. As this implies, I would walk from department to department, not "checking up," but being present. Employees like to see the boss. They will work a little harder when they know someone is watching. This is human nature. I did not walk around yelling at people. I simply encouraged and occasionally pushed a little. Plus, people like to be seen doing a good job as well.

From books, movies, jobs, and life we all know both great and not-so-great leaders. Observe the good ones; study just how they act and react in many situations. For a few, good leadership just comes naturally. But for most of us, it has to be learned. The most important thing is that you are hard-working, ethical, and confident of the goals, mission, and direction of your organization. If this is the case, you will be a great leader.

50

Appearance

When you are the leader of a company, you must look and act like a president at all times. Read the book *Dress for Success;* it's a great guide for grooming and attire. In 1992, I required all TSI men to wear suits and ties all the time and women to wear suits or blazers and skirts.

We were providing businesses with one of their most important assets. Computers are serious business. Every company in the world depends on computers. From the smallest to the biggest company, most can't run at all if their computer systems are down. From selling to manufacturing to shipping, customer data is all on computers. When computers are down, nothing can be completed. Time is lost and time is money.

I went to a restaurant recently and the doors were locked and a sign read, "Computers down, closed for the day." A few days later, I was back and I asked the owner about it.

I said, "You could still have cooked me a burger and fries."

He replied, "The staff wouldn't have been able to access or retrieve inventory, price the meal, or charge you for it."

Because TSI's business supported critical information, I always felt we should dress like bankers, lawyers, accountants, and other similar professionals. If your business is tied to college students, dress the part. If you are selling to the "high-fashion" industry, you'd better dress the part as well.

As business changed over the years along with fashion, I realized it was okay to wear a sports coat and dress down a little. Even so, every employee was required to look professional.

We had the Chrysler Corporation as a client, and they asked our sales executives *not* to wear blue suits and ties. They claimed when our guys came in, everyone thought they were the auditors sniffing around. So my guys dressed down for these meeting. However, we had a client in western Michigan, Gordon Foods, and they were all in suits and ties. So our staff in both sales and technology wore suits and ties when they made visits or sales calls to the company.

You must consider your own situation to set the right policy. Base it on your products, customers, or the area in which you live. But have a written dress code that is clear. It should be in your company policy handbook. Your dress code should be discussed with potential new employees long before you hire them. Some people feel how they present themselves and what they wear is their personal right; true, but not while they are on the clock working for you. We hired a lot of people fresh out of college and sometimes we had to "educate" them about the real world. They were no longer at college where they could wear whatever they wanted and express themselves in their attire. They were now part of corporate America and had to fit in. You should also think through beards, hair length, and general grooming as well, then set a specific policy in these areas. Whatever decisions you make in this area, make sure it's crystal clear and in your company handbook. Also every employee as a condition of employment with your company must read and sign an acknowledgment of the handbook. This will save you a lot of discussion, hassle, and debating.

51

Ethics

"There is no such thing as a minor lapse of integrity."
—Tom Peters,
American writer on business management

Sound ethics, in general, is a critical requirement for entrepreneurs. We all are judged by our actions. The way you behave and act will lead people to conclusions about you as a person and as a leader.

Cheating, stealing, and lying should never be tolerated by anyone, especially a leader, founder, or president. Trust and honesty will build a solid organization. The opposite will destroy the organization overnight. You may get away with something once or twice, but you will know it was wrong and it will haunt you and will likely catch up to you as well. However, the moral consequence of your indiscretion is never going to pay off. My father told me as a young man that one lie leads to another and another. Remembering a lie is impossible. The golden rule is one of the best. Never tell a lie, period. And once you learn that someone has lied to you, what do you think? Once a liar, always a liar.

A person's character is important at all times.

I remember that shortly after TSI was formed, we completed a contract for a very large corporation. Our invoice amount was for $28,500, and we received a check for $285,000. In the beginning

I always opened up all the mail. Upon seeing this check, I knew instantly that it was a computer error. The organization probably ran millions of dollars in checks each week.

Who would know? My mind swirled around a realm of possibilities. We could really use the cash flow. This would be a tremendous windfall of needed cash and profits. Plus, the corporation would never know. If they caught the error, I could always blame our financial department. Mistakes happen after all, and all would be forgiven.

I showed my partner, Mark, the check along with the invoice. We both smiled, and he asked what I was going to do. After the fleeting thoughts of needed equipment, lavish meals, plus a cool trip or two danced in my mind for ten seconds, I turned to Mark and said, "Watch what I'm going to do."

I called the accounts-payable department of this public company and, after being transferred all over the place, I finally got a real live person. I advised him of the error and then returned the check. We did a lot of business with this company over the years. They may have or may not have ever figured out the mistake. But to keep the check would have been stealing, period.

The individuals we are today are the result of many things: upbringing, education, genetics, experience, and the decisions we make. Make the right and ethical decision every time.

Over the years, our company received many checks for the wrong amount, amazing to me. My financial department clearly knew my requirement. Correct the matter, and return any amount not due to us.

As a leader, you must demonstrate and demand ethical practices. A cheater will never prosper in the long term.

Think for a moment about someone you know who demonstrates good ethical behavior all the time. Now think of someone you may know who does not. If both of these individuals ran a company, which one would you want to work for and be affiliated with? Simple question.

52

Relationships

"Be aware of the dangers of the supermarket syndrome."

—Robert H. Gotshall Sr.

At one of our Friday lunches, I explained to my dad how I had the opportunity to use somebody for my good but at that person's expense. I described how I would probably get away with it. Plus, I would probably never see the person again.

My dad responded, "Just when you think you will get away with it, the supermarket syndrome will kick your butt."

Over the years, my dad had many strange things to explain, but this time I figured he was a little off. So I bit, "What's the supermarket syndrome?"

He said, "Close your eyes and visualize a typical supermarket. Now, describe just what you see."

I told him I saw row after row of endless products piled to the ceiling.

"Now, you are walking down one of these aisles," my dad continued. "You are about halfway down the aisle when you see the person you screwed over coming down the aisle toward you. What are you going to do? Jump up and over the shelves of food? I don't think so. You are stuck with coming face-to-face with this person.

You are a trapped rat. Embarrassed and caught and forced to face the music. Not worth it . . . is it?"

In business, there are many opportunities to do the right or wrong thing. Sometimes the temptation is great to go down the "bad" path. But it's just not worth it. It will create bad feelings and someday you will be caught in the supermarket aisle. Just like business ethics, there are people ethics. And you must treat everyone in an honorable way at all times.

53

Zany, Crazy, and Remaining Respectable

This is a strange topic for entrepreneurs. We are the grounded ones, leading our organizations. We are viewed as the rock, always serious and in control. True for the most part. However, there is a fine line you may cross when the time is right. During the work day, it's important to maintain a certain level of decorum. You should be respectable. You are not to be the class clown, bully, or hard ass. That said, there is a time and place for even you to show a different side of yourself.

One of the best things I did in front of my employees happened at a Detroit Tigers Opening Day outing. I loved to hold events that created camaraderie among my employees and vendors that were fun. It's essential in all companies to have some fun.

So every year, our marketing director purchased a block of tickets for the Tiger's Opening Day game. We would rent a big travel coach bus, invite a few select vendors along with the entire company, and go to the baseball game. I provided breakfast and off we would go for the day. This was a TSI holiday for everyone. We would even have a few beers on the bus and pre-party.

At one of the games, the peanut vendor was making his way down the aisle, yelling: "Peanuts, get your peanuts . . . peanuts, get 'em while they're hot . . ." I stopped this guy and said, "Can I take over for you?" He looked at me like I was crazy, but then replied,

"Sure . . . Why not?" So I put on his large over-the-shoulder satchel with all the individual peanut bags in it.

And then I proclaimed in my best baseball game vendor loud voice, "Peanuts, get 'em while they're hot . . . Peanuts . . . who needs Peanuts?"

I soon had sixty of my employees and vendors all cheering and screaming for a bag. So I started tossing bags of peanuts to all of them. Well, this got a lot of attention from everyone in the section. They all wanted in on the fun as well. I tossed out 100 bags of peanuts to my employees, vendors, and a number of complete strangers. The TV cameras even had this whole scene on national TV. At one point, because of the wild crowd, two Detroit police officers made their way down the aisle to make sure a riot was not breaking out. They asked both the real peanut vendor and me what was going on.

I quickly assured the police officers that I was prepared to pay for the entire peanut supply and I was not drunk. The vendor, sensing a large tip coming his way, also said everything was under control. Now with the police there and my employees and the surrounding fans all going crazy, it was quite a scene. After the satchel was empty, the section gave me a standing ovation. I took my bow, paid the vendor for the peanuts plus a handsome tip, and took my seat.

People who were sitting around us asked a number of my staff who I was and what had just happened. They explained that I was the company president and we came to Opening Day every year. Again and again, people said, "How do I get a job at your company?"

I never made a fool out of myself, and I know everyone had a great time. Years later, employees who had attended that particular Opening Day still talked about the event with great fondness and appreciation.

Make the effort to let your employees know you are fun and someone other than a boss. During social outings, let down your guard a bit while retaining your dignity.

54

Self-Preservation

Burnout is tough to recover from. You should work like hell, but you must manage your personal life as well. To keep fresh, you must "turn it off" at times and focus on the rest of your life. In the beginning, I didn't do this very well.

However, after three years of working sixty-plus hours a week, I became numb.

My dad would say, "All work and no play makes Tommy boring."

That is why it is important to have faith, family, and friends along with hobbies. One's faith is personal. However, I joined the church when I was an adult. Why? Although I was raised a Methodist and had officially joined the church at age thirteen, I went less and less after that.

Faith

My parents didn't feel strongly about it, so I, like so many, drifted away. The only time I went to church with them was for a wedding or funeral (the WF syndrome).

My wife, Marti, was a strong Catholic when we met, and her family is very religious. All eight of her brothers and sisters went to Catholic schools from kindergarten through twelfth grade. Even up north at the family compound, the question was: "What time are you going to mass this weekend?"

I knew that becoming Catholic would strengthen both my faith and my relationship with Marti and her entire family. Good family building, I figured.

Growing up, most if not all of us have no say in what religion we subscribe to. Parents dictate this 100 percent.

At twenty-seven, I became a Catholic. It was a tremendous experience. The priest decided it didn't make sense for me to attend a class with a bunch of thirteen-year-olds, so he designed a special program for me. I was assigned to a deacon. Each week, the deacon would give me a book to read, and the following week, we would talk about it. As an adult, reading and studying all aspects of different faiths was very interesting and eye opening. I have been told that the best Catholics are the converts because they made the choice as an adult to join the faith.

Again, one's faith is personal. However, we all need "some higher spirit" to talk to at times. This is very true for the entrepreneur. It is very lonely at the top. Many times, you will need "someone" to talk things over with. Be comfortable with this. Plus, sometimes you will need to pray for guidance or inspiration.

My point is, reach out and have those "conversations" whenever you need to. They are always private. If you are not at the point to have a spiritual connection with God, I would recommend that you find someone who can be your confidant and sounding board.

Family

Family is everything. Being involved and attentive to your family will be the most important thing you will do in this life. Hands down!

Make time for your family. I coached all my kids in their respective sports, from the time they were four years old through high school. When my kids were in high school, I attended every tennis match and volleyball game along with lacrosse and football games. Often, I would go back to the office after a game and work late. But I was always there for my family.

Those years pass way too fast. Blink and the kids are off to college. There are no do-overs when it comes to kids. Your work and success as an entrepreneur will provide many benefits to your family; however, your involvement with all aspects of their lives trumps work every time. Make sure you are there for the important stuff. Also, there is nothing like family vacations. Going somewhere together and enjoying each other will provide great lifelong memories as well as recharge your batteries. And remember, don't allow work distractions and calls to cut into this very important time together.

My kids, Kristen, T.J., and Erica,
on Mackinac Island, 2013

Hobbies

Also, it's important to have a hobby yourself. Mine is golf. I didn't start playing until I was twenty-three. In high school, I didn't think golf was cool, too bad for me. My dad also loved golf. After I started to play, we had many outings together. One of my goals was to have enough money to join a country club, which after saving for years I finally did. I took lessons and played on Saturday or Sunday with my pals.

My dad told me that playing golf was the best way to get to know someone. The sport is also a great way to interact with customers. I never played during the week unless it was with a customer. The four hours on the course plus a drink after provided plenty of opportunities to get close to a customer or vendor. Getting that amount of time with a key executive or decision maker is otherwise impossible. I never talked business on the course unless someone else brought it up. This time allowed us to get to know each other and greatly improved our business relationship. You learn a lot about someone on the golf course because the game requires some athletic ability plus honesty, integrity, and knowledge. This will also tell your customer about who you are. Never, ever cheat. If you feel the other players want a break, give it to them. Do Not lecture them about the rules; remember this is not the U.S. Open. Your role is to develop a better relationship and more business. There are many other activities you can enjoy with a client: hunting, fishing, or attending an event. The key is to spend some time away from the office and confines of the business environment and get to know them better.

Health

I am not a doctor, but we all know stress can kill you. Heart attacks happen to men and women of all ages these days.

Taking care of your health is a requirement. You must deal with stress. It's in all of our lives. But for the entrepreneur there is ten times more stress. The pressure of running a business is unreal. Employee issues, customer issues, decisions to make.

Rid yourself of stress. I relieve it by getting away, mentally. I love golf, so I go hit golf balls at lunch. I get unplugged from it all. Escape. The issue will exist when you go back, but a break from it all is good and time away can even help you develop a new solution. Others work out (two benefits), go for a walk, read, or do other things that they find relaxing, just for a little break.

At work, learn how to make decisions and don't dwell endlessly on problems. You will make a lot of decisions; some small, some major.

Take time to weigh all aspects of a situation. Look at all the ramifications of the potential conclusions; then commit to a final decision, and move on. From a very young age, we are called on to make decisions.

As an entrepreneur, you will make decisions that will affect many people. You must be comfortable with this process and master it from the beginning. Stick to your guns and don't be wishy-washy. It's okay to get input from others; however, in the end you alone must make the final decision.

Take your time but make a decision and move on.

Don't take your work home. Whatever time you finish, go home and forget about it as best as you can. Taking this downtime will go far in helping you maintain, or achieve, good health.

55

To Sell or Not to Sell

When you start a company, the farthest thing from your mind is probably selling it. And some never consider selling. However, this should be a primary reason for starting a business in the first place. You might not ever sell, but keep this possibility in mind anyway.

If you choose to sell, the two key questions are when to sell and how to sell.

Taking an idea from concept to successful completion makes you very attached to it. Certainly not like a child, but it becomes part of you nonetheless. People will associate you with your company. You will think about it all the time. How to improve it, change it, and make it better. You will take great pride with its success, and any failure will make you miserable.

However, the bottom line is the bottom line. It depends on just what you want out of it all. I thought long and hard about selling my company, TSI. *Should I keep it going for my kids?*

This is a difficult question to answer. Many second-generation businesses do poorly, simple because the next generation has little or no interest in the business. It depends generally on the age of the kids and their interest. If they are young and especially under the age of twenty-one, who knows what they will want to do.

On the other hand, there are many successful second- and third-generation companies. I know a fourth-generation coffee manufacturing company that does very well. The current president,

Nick, loves the business and has a strong interest in improving and growing it.

However, after running my company for eighteen years, I knew it was time to sell the entire company. Note, I previously had sold half the company, in 2003.

Timing is everything. We had just had two great years in a row, plus venture capital and private equity firms were out buying many companies just like TSI.

I did a lot of research. I found a ton of information on the Internet. I also talked with lawyers and accountants, because a seller must have a good understanding of all the tax and legal ramifications of the transaction.

If a company is distressed and losing money, the owner may have no choice but to sell. However, this is not a great time to unload. The sharks see blood in the water.

If you decide to move forward with the sale of your company, this will potentially be the biggest financial deal in your life.

Getting the Best Advice

Legal advice: Do your homework. If you have a lawyer who is a generalist, don't ask this professional to complete the deal. This professional may be great at a variety of legal matters but not this specialization.

You need an M & A attorney (merger and acquisition) with experience. When selecting the law firm, keep the following in mind:

- Consider at least three firms.
- Interview each of them with a set of specific questions.
- Find out how many transactions they have completed.
- Find out if they have represented both the selling firm and the buying firm. It is best if they know both sides of the equation.

Do they charge by the hour or do you pay a set price for a completed deal? Usually it will be a hybrid of this, an upfront cost, plus time and material. Ask for a ballpark figure with a cap on it.

I would recommend working with a large firm in your area. A small firm would love to do your transaction, but you don't want a generalist handling the most important financial deal of your life.

If you belong to a CEO roundtable group, this is a great place to get a reference. Or, if you know someone who has sold his or her company, all the better. A proven success story is always the best way to find representation.

After you have selected the firm, ask your attorney a lot of questions about the types of things that will come up in the sales process. This will tell you about his or her level of experience; plus, you will gain much insight into the process.

Next, find a business broker. Use the same criteria as when you were looking for an attorney:

- Experience
- Industry worked in
- How they operate
- Cost
- What size deals they usually do

You want someone who has closed deals in your size range. The first firm I hired was in Atlanta. Most of the companies they represented had revenue of $300 million.

My company had revenue of $30 million. My little deal didn't get any attention within their firm. Also, every time they traveled to Michigan, I paid all the expenses. They always traveled first-class and stayed in the best hotels. This cost me $4,000 each time and they never completed a deal.

Also, be prepared to pay an upfront retainer fee. Usually, this fee will go toward their firm preparing a book or a marketing piece about your company. The "book" is used to present your company to prospective buyers. It will include

- Financials
- Business history
- Organizational chart
- Resumés on key employees
- Mission statement

It will also include revenue along with profit projections for the next one, three, and five years. Be careful with this one. Some transactions will be tied to these "future" results. Be positive and conservative. This must represent growth. Can you justify this projection? You will be required to justify your projections with concrete reasoning. Ask to see an example of a book they prepared for another client. This will tell you a lot about just how they market a firm.

Experience is critical in selling your company. The firm may be experienced at selling manufacturing companies but may not be knowledgeable about how to sell in your market segment. All selling is not the same. For example, selling a technology company is completely different from selling a wholesale distribution firm. The financial metrics, evaluation, the buyers, and earn outs are all different. Do not let someone use your deal to learn about your industry.

Firms will also charge a success fee. This will be a flat amount along with an additional percentage based on the selling price. A schedule of this fee must be put in writing and be crystal clear from the start. You will be required to sign documents with both the legal firm and business broker. Make sure you completely understand what you are signing in both cases.

Also, check to see how long the contract runs. Is it exclusive? What if you find the buyer? Usually, you will still pay the commission. If you want to exclude a few potential buyers, you must have this in writing. A typical contract will run for six months. Obviously these decisions are big, so do your research and take your time.

56

Exiting

Beware of the Buyer

Selling your company can be a dream come true, or it can be a nightmare.

The good, the bad, and the ugly.

The good deal is a simple, straightforward transaction. All cash at closing. However, rare these days.

Once you start down the path of selling your company, you will be very excited. But hold your emotions in check. You still have a company to run.

First off, tell no one you are potentially selling the company, period. Just because you feel it is the best thing for you, does not mean that holds true for anyone else. In fact, it is the opposite.

Your loyal employees will be scared to death that you will depart the company with a bagful of money, leaving them to deal with some unknown big bad new set of owners. Also, all your vendors and bankers will assume the new firm will strip the company. Sometimes that does happen, but it's usually not the case.

Nothing good will come of the news on the street that you, the founder and guiding beacon of the company, are sailing off to bask in the sunshine of retirement. Plus, often you will be staying on at the company after it is sold. But still, everyone will assume you are gone.

If your business broker is experienced, he or she will have potential buyers lined up at the beginning of the sales process. Otherwise, the broker should have an interested party identified within thirty days or less.

During the sales cycle, prospective buyers will want to meet you and see your operation. This may be a little tricky, but do everything you can to keep this potential information from others. If you could meet off site, even better. In this meeting with the prospective buyers, you will get a variety of questions. Be prepared for everything. Typical questions:

- Why are you selling?
- Do you want to stay on?
- Give us "your" history of the company.
- Tell us about your key employees.
- What is your expected revenue and profits growth for the next one, three, and five years?
- Detail your company's typical transaction.
- Tell us about your top three accounts.
- What are the strengths and weaknesses in your company?
- How much do you want and in what structure?
- Tell us about your competition.

Your broker should review all of these anticipated questions with you in advance. A mock presentation and question and answer session is a good idea.

Be positive, but don't BS any aspect of your business. The ideal situation is for you to have two or even three potential buyers in the process simultaneously. That way, you can pick the best one to proceed with but also have a backup. Usually, the top pick will request that you enter into an exclusive contract to negotiate only with them for some period of time, usually thirty or sixty days.

In this process, they will pick apart all aspects of your company. They will request an endless amount of information. I hired an outside consultant to prepare for and respond to all of this. It took two months to complete this task.

The buyer will make an initial offer and, after this process, will probably modify it somewhat.

> Remember: Cash is king. Beware of stock as valuable consideration.
> Desired result: Most or all the cash at closing.

However, most buyers will want to hold back a portion for some period, perhaps six months to three years. Any money held back should carry an interest payment to you that is paid each month.

Also, some will want to tie this note to performance. It's best not to do this because you don't know what the future will bring. That is why your projections should be well thought out.

Is the note payment to be taken out of the proceeds of the business? What if the company is losing money under the new management and "can't afford" the note? This is why you start with a very good attorney.

If you get stock in the new company (New Co), what conditions come with it? Are you subject to a cash call if the company is losing money? Is your stock preferred or common?

Your attorney will play a huge part in negotiating all of this— another reason it is critical to have the best one at your side.

After closing on the sale of your company, take a big breath and celebrate. Now you must advise a number of important parties.

Advising employees: Be very positive and inform them that this will be best for them. That is all the care about, Do not discuss the financial details of the transaction. It is nobody's business.

Your bank: Call them and tell them the same. However, they will probably already know about the sale.

Your CPA: You should have talked about all the tax ramifications with him or her already.

Your customers and vendors: Prepare an upbeat, positive press release.

There will be some surprises in this process; trust me. After I sold my company, the company that I no longer owned got a bill for $400,000. I was told by the private equity firm that this was the processing fee for the deal. This was their way of taking cash out of the business. Also, they charged a "management" fee of $30,000 a month. I asked, "For what?"

Again, I had to remember I no longer owned the business. It was their company now and these types of decisions were their decisions to make, even though I still worked there. My attorney told me these fees were excessive, but typical.

While I was retained to run the company, the new owners were now calling all the shots. This was difficult for me at first, though I completely understood this was just how private equity firms operate.

Once your company is sold, the purchasers will establish an "authority matrix" (AM) that sets forth how the business will be run. All decisions will follow a specific set of sign-offs. For example, say you want to hire another sales executive. You will have to write up a justification and provide a compensation plan for this new person. You may also be required to have two directors at the firm approve the plan. If you need to purchase a new copier, same thing: a justification with cost and the appropriate sign-offs. This AM will be your new bible for operations. You must adapt to it or leave the company. Make sure to think this through before you sell your company.

For me, the payoff to starting my company was to sell it and move on to another project.

Consider the following when contemplating selling your company:

1. Reoccurring and predictable revenue and profits will bring the greatest selling value.
2. Most buyers will want to keep you on as president because "you are the business."
3. Be conservative, but positive, with your forecast.
4. Timing is everything.
5. Cash is king.
6. Hire the best team of lawyers, accountants, and business brokers you can.
7. Be over-prepared for all questions from prospective buyers.
8. Keep everything confidential before, during, and even after the sale of your company. The terms and selling price of your company should remain confidential.
9. If you are emotionally attached to your company and the potential money you will earn does not feel like it is important, do not sell.

57

Creating Your Grand Future

"The difference between a successful person
and others is not a lack of strength, not a lack of
knowledge, but a lack of will."

—Vince Lombardi,
Green Bay Packers coach

At times you may lose faith and feel that your entrepreneurial
dream will never come to fruition. From just starting your venture
to the first few months there are real obstacles. When you encounter
these obstacles, take a short pause, regroup, and move on. It would be
easy to just pack it in and quit. Think of all the great and successful
entrepreneurs and know that they, too, were at this challenging point
many times and yet forged on. It was not easy for any of them either.
Close your eyes and imagine yourself as this incredibly successful
entrepreneur. Great vision! It will be worth it, I know. Now get back
to work and start creating your grand future. Just about everything
great in the world was envisioned, created, and followed through by
an individual entrepreneur. You can also be that unique and special
person if you so choose.

You will be required to have a strong will along with unwavering
commitment. Do not allow anyone to get you off track. And, above
all, believe in yourself and your destiny.

Epilogue

My ending should be your beginning.

My original objective in writing this book was to find a release. Dealing with the death of my dad was very hard and somehow writing about our lifelong adventure helped me. Along the way, I hope I have inspired you and provided guidance you can use in your entrepreneurial quest. Do not let my book's conclusion be your conclusion as well. Take action now and plan for the rest of your life. It will be hard work, but the work will be well worth it. What I found is that the life of an entrepreneur is a fascinating journey. An entrepreneur must be willing to take on any task or challenge, no matter how insignificant or grand. An entrepreneur's attitude must at all times be positive and up to any required challenge. The rewards can be endless. An entrepreneur will be called on to make decisions about issues he or she is not currently aware of and deal with a wide assortment of situations. But that is the beauty of the quest.

Remember, keep your eye on the goal.

The true "secret sauce" is in the experience of being an entrepreneur. The process of doing will teach you how to be a great entrepreneur. You must be passionate about the quest and run with your instincts. Each day you will learn something new, and tomorrow you will be a better entrepreneur for it.

I am proof that becoming a successful entrepreneur can happen for most anybody. I had a great advantage that no one else had, my dad. However, now you have his wisdom, thoughts, and positive outlook as well.

Please start today; make your plans and goals. Write them down with dates. Take control of your destination and stay on course.

Good luck, stay focused, and build your enterprise. You will have a positive impact on an endless array of people you don't even know today.

As for me, entrepreneurship is in my bones. I have a few new projects I'm contemplating now. And I hope you will see them or read about them in the future.